Praise for *Practical Mysticism* . . .

"David Samuel's *Practical Mysticism* is an exciting blend of ancient traditional wisdom and modern applications. This book offers a great opportunity to work with an obvious master of manifestation, whose clarity and spiritual integrity shines through on every page in a delightfully accessible presentation."

–Carol Adrienne, PhD
Author of *The Purpose of Your Life*

"Yoking together an enormous amount of knowledge from various paths and cultures, Samuel has created a well-researched, intimate and perceptive guide for maintaining spirituality in everyday life. . . . This quietly spoken book rapidly gets to the heart of problems, emotions, business concerns. . . . Many, many suggestions here—for making decisions, clarifying goals, choosing positive thoughts and keeping logic clear. There is weight and substance in *Practical Mysticism,* and a quiet and tenacious majesty."

–*The Book Reader*

"David has artfully and practically bridged the world of business and the world of spirit, validating what we know intuitively to be true: material success and spiritual attunement are two sides of one coin."

–Nancy Rosanoff
Author of *The Complete Idiots' Guide to Making Money through Intuition and Intuition Workout*

"*Practical Mysticism* will help readers find their spiritual way amidst their daily life. This broad-reaching and thought-provoking guide will bring blessings into the world. I recommend it heartily to whoever strives to live in this world without being totally overcome by it."

–Lama Surya Das
Author of *Awakening to the Sacred*

"*Practical Mysticism* is fascinating, instructional and deeply satisfying for all of us longing to manifest the perennial philosophy in our life and work."

–Stan Madson, Co-Owner, Bodhi Tree Bookstore
(West Hollywood Chamber of Commerce Business of the Year 1999) and Publisher, *Bodhi Tree Book Review*

Practical
Mysticism

**Business Success and Balanced Living through
Ancient and Modern Spiritual Teachings**

David Samuel

Foreword by Robert Frager, Ph.D.

BP

Bakshi Publications, LLC
Denver, Colorado

Published by: Bakshi Publications, LLC
              283 Columbine Street, Suite 123
              Denver, CO 80206

Editor: Ellen Kleiner
Book design and production: Orbit Design
Cover design and production: Foster & Foster

Printed in the United States of America on acid-free recycled paper

Publisher's Cataloging-in-Publication Data

Samuel, David, 1961–
      Practical mysticism : business success and balanced
      living through ancient and modern spiritual teachings /
      David Samuel. — 1st ed.
            p. cm.
            Includes bibliographical references.
            LCCN: 99-90376
            ISBN: 0-9671384-0-X

      1. Mysticism. 2. Spiritual life—New Age
      movement. 3. Self-help techniques. 4. Success in
      business. I. Title.

  BL625.S26 1999   291.4'22
                        QBI99-659

10 9 8 7 6 5 4 3 2 1

This book is dedicated to:

All my teachers, especially the late Sufi master
Sheikh Safer Dal Efendi, of Istanbul, who with all his love
and wisdom told me, "If you have a skill, it is your duty to teach";

My brother Michael, a scholar knowledgeable in many traditions,
who has been an endless source of information, help, and encouragement;

And my students, from whom I have gained so much and who asked
the questions that brought this material into written form.

"I have learned much from my teachers,
even more from my colleagues,
and most of all from my students."
—The Babylonian Talmud

Acknowledgments

I would like to express my deep appreciation to Ellen Kleiner, who was so generous with her time and efforts while editing and guiding me in publishing this first book.

"If" by Rudyard Kipling from *Kipling: Victorian Balladeer,* published by Gramercy Books, used by permission of A.P. Watt Ltd on behalf of The National Trust for Places of Historic Interest or Natural Beauty.

Contents

I. Self-Discovery

II. The Worldly Side of Life

III. Psychological and Emotional Refinement

IV. Self-Cultivation

Foreword

An old Sufi definition of a spiritual teacher is "a mature person who has been 'cooked' (by the ups and downs of living in the world)." Through his rich and varied experiences, David Samuel has been cooked. He understands practical mysticism firsthand, as he has successfully applied in his own life the principles and practices he presents.

I was very fortunate to have been exposed at a young age to many of the ideas covered in *Practical Mysticism*. In my mid-twenties, I lived in Japan and studied with my first spiritual teacher. Master Tempu Nakamura had been spiritual tutor to the Imperial Family and was a spiritual teacher to many prominent Japanese intellectuals, scientists, politicians, and business leaders. He was a living illustration of the power of positive attitudes and effective goal setting. In his early nineties, Master Tempu looked like a youthful fifty year old and had the energy of someone in his twenties. He was an inspiring philosopher and psychologist, and also a gifted artist, calligrapher, lecturer, and writer. One great lesson I learned from him was that our only real limits are those we place on ourselves.

The principles of Practical Mysticism form a perennial psychology, a psychology that has been independently discovered by many successful men and women. For years I have taught seminars in these universal principles to hundreds of men and women ranging from college students to heads of large corporations, from blue-collar workers to doctors, lawyers, and judges. Based on my personal experience as well as the experience of my students, I know these basic practices and principles work; they are extremely effective if you use them.

One of the basic messages of this book is to take responsibility for your life. Too many people let themselves drift through life like a boat with no one at the helm. Then if they fail to build a fulfilling life, they blame their childhood, society, genes, or bad luck. The following pages present many practical techniques we can use to *change* our lives. We can change old habits; we can learn effective ways to achieve our most important goals; we can also enjoy financial abundance. And we can learn to deeply nourish mind, body, and soul.

My own Sufi master, Safer Efendi, was also David Samuel's teacher. With the most beautiful humility, Safer Efendi once remarked, "What little I know of Sufism is what I have loved and practiced for over forty years." To learn anything deeply you have to love it and practice it. If you sincerely practice the techniques presented in this book, you will learn a great deal. They might even transform your life.

This book has been inspired in many ways by the Sufi mystical tradition. Sufism has flourished throughout the world, especially in Europe, Africa, the Middle East, and Asia. Throughout its 1,500-year-old history, it has provided great examples of deep spiritual attainment coupled with active engagement in the world. Sufism is not a retreatist or an elitist tradition; indeed, Sufi teachers have included laborers, fishermen, artisans, and merchants as well as scholars, poets, and philosophers. My own Sufi teachers have raised families and run businesses, or pursued professional careers. *All* their life experiences have been integral parts of their spiritual journeys.

Sufism teaches that to seek God you do not need to change your life or quit your job. You do not need to become a vegetarian or embrace celibacy. You do need to begin to open your heart and practice greater love, compassion, and awareness in your life as it is *right now*. Once these first changes are made, who knows where they will lead you?

The tools presented in *Practical Mysticism* are deceptively simple-seeming. However, in order to make a serious commitment to use them, you need to believe that you have the capacity to change and to develop the kind of life you want. I know you have this capacity, and so does David Samuel. (After all, that's why he wrote this book!) Now it is up to you.

Robert Frager, Ph.D.
Founding president and professor of psychology at the Institute of
Transpersonal Psychology and the author of Heart, Self, & Soul

Preface

I was born to a lower-middle-class family, went to work at age twelve, and started my first business at age thirteen. Using the principles in this book, I became a self-made millionaire by twenty-five and was able to retire at twenty-eight. I lived in Montreal, Canada, until I retired, and then I left on an extended journey of spiritual discovery. Wandering around the world for several years, I visited over thirty countries, carrying nothing more than my backpack and with no agenda other than to learn from my experiences. I would simply wake up each day and decide on a destination, with no thought until that evening about where I would sleep—whether in a comfortable hotel or outside on the ground.

I left home heading west and returned from the east. In California, I saw giant redwood trees twenty stories high and wide as a house. In Hawaii, it was volcanoes and black sand—landscapes like the moon. In Japan, I saw Mount Fuji, a perfect pyramid; a medley of Kyoto's 2,000 temples; the largest wooden building in the world, surrounding an immense Buddha cast in bronze; and Hiroshima, recovered from atomic devastation yet with pain still in the air. I traveled by boat in the Sea of Japan as a typhoon approached, walked on a grumbling and steaming volcano, and lived the life of a Zen monk in peaceful isolation.

In Taipei, home of money and power on the little island of Taiwan, I found Taoist masters in hidden corners. In the northern hill villages of Thailand, I met people surviving only on the resources the jungle provided. In the bustling city of Bangkok, I laid eyes on the Emerald Buddha in its gold and jeweled palace. Farther south, the fine white powdered sand of beaches squeaked under my feet. There I swam in oceans still and clear, and visited temples, palaces, ancient holy places, each one a universe of its own.

In India, I saw the Taj Mahal; sunrise on the Ganges; New Delhi with its pillar made of a material none can date or define; a Rolls-Royce waiting alongside an elephant at a Bombay traffic light; the ten-story-high Elephanta and Ellora cave temples carved out of a mountain, with paintings hundreds of years old still vividly colored; the temples of Khajuraho, decorated from top to bottom with erotic stone carvings. I traveled by camel through the Rajasthan desert, sleeping under the stars and seeing nothing but sand for days on end, alone yet so close to God I did not feel lonely.

From the start I met innumerable types of people—some with nothing but an ever-present smile, others with millions of dollars and a frown. Shamans, Zen masters, gurus, the Dalai Lama, and a passenger on a train who saw right through me, offering wise words when I was down and lost. I encountered poverty and riches, death and health, portions of a corpse floating past my boat on the holy Ganges River while a local drank from the water. I watched people shot to death and, on the same street, others who honored the life of a fly.

In Turkey, I was robbed and left without enough change for so much as a phone call. That night, in the local police station, I saw how officers beat captured thieves, though they showered me with incomparable compassion, giving me food, money, and shelter. The next day, a complete rainbow over a mountain lake renewed my faith that all would be well.

In Egypt, I saw the Great Pyramids, King Tut in his tomb, the Valley of the Kings, temples cut hundreds of feet into rocky mountains. One, still in perfect condition after 7,000 years, was beginning to show telltale signs of pollution. Another, the temple of Abu Simbel, is now a feat of the ancient ones who built it as well as the modern men who moved it—along with the mountain encasing it—to save it from flooding by the Aswan High Dam.

Modern man reshapes the planet to suit himself, forming wonders of art, ingenuity, and pure inspiration. The Goddard tunnel, seventeen kilometers long, drilled through a mountain in the Swiss Alps. Walls going up in Cyprus, coming down in Berlin, and Stonehenge still standing. The man-made creations I pondered in amazement; the God-made ones took my breath away.

In the Middle East, I saw the Dead Sea with no life in it and, only hours away, the Red Sea teeming with occupants of various colors, shapes, and sizes. In the desert by Mount Sinai stand five tall, strong Cyprus trees, which have marked a source of fresh water for centuries. I climbed the mountain, as did Moses, and slept on the rock at its peak.

Gods of all sorts crossed my path. Nature spirits in Hawaii; a giant phallus in Japan; the elephant-headed Ganesh, one of India's 10,000 deities; and crocodiles in Egypt. Brighter than them all was the love and devotion of the people who honor them. That love is the true God.

In tiny Belize, I explored Mayan temples. On nearby beaches adventurous souls could live freely in lean-tos made of grass, eating fruit from the trees and fish from the ocean.

Animals were everywhere. Rhinos with armorlike skin in the jungles of Nepal; eagles soaring through the sky over the Himalayas; painted elephants; a lone baby seal on a deserted beach; tigers and varieties of monkeys; peacocks and parrots; tiny fluorescent blue-green insects; the amazing metamorphosis of a caterpillar into a butterfly.

I experienced the many moods of nature. Rugged mountains giving way to rolling hills and fields. Miles of flatlands ending abruptly in 10,000-foot peaks that stand guard to heaven. Scottish skies so full of shifting shapes I thought I was watching a film. A Himalayan thunderstorm rising from the valley below, then bombarding the mountain with huge hailstones. The sun, glowing orange from behind a cloud, sending out a bright golden aura in all directions—reminding me that although the sun can be hidden it can never be extinguished. A sunbeam touched me like a warm hand, enlightening me about nature's power within us all. Its power could be seen in flowers of royal purple, vibrant blues, firelike yellows, oranges, and reds, as well as pure white; and in tiny dots of open petals and long slender cups looking upward or hanging shyly down.

Nature's power also radiated from children everywhere, smiling with joy and warmth. When I was losing strength, the hug of a child filled me with sustenance—given, as it was, out of pure love, without question or reserve.

I have climbed the Alps and the Himalayas, so high up that airplanes flew below me; I've walked alone in isolated lands so peaceful that butterflies landed on my arms; I've ridden in a submarine beneath the sea. On the earth and in my soul, I've touched the greatest heights and depths. Years spent wandering the planet, looking deep within by seeing what was without, I have cried tears for myself and others, including those who may not know of suffering or appreciate their blessed lives.

Although I am growing older, I feel cleaner and lighter every day. For now I know that we are all a creation of the divine, that our personalities have been molded by the country we live in, and that our quest is to return to the divine beings we were created to be. From a seed, I grew and was then picked and woven into the man I am. The day will come when I shall be left somewhere, my body returning to the earth, my soul traveling freely like the wind. Knowing we are One, I am not afraid.

Aware that the power to find our destiny is within each of us, and is something we must see for ourselves, I continually await the next adventure. My quest begins anew each morning.

*   *   *

While roaming the world on my spiritual search, I participated in meditation groups and studied Zen, Buddhism, Taoism, Sufism, the works of Gurdjieff and P. D. Ouspensky, as well as many other spiritual practices. I attended schools that specialize in these teachings and came back to form a school of my own, applying the insights to modern-day Western life and business, as well as to personal and spiritual growth. At times in my travels, I was so socially active I'd have to book lunch with a friend three weeks in advance. At other times, I spent extended periods as a hermit, practicing Tai Chi, Qi Gong, and meditation by day, then reading spiritual texts on into the night, devoid of human contact except while purchasing groceries and other necessities.

Looking for the missing links in my path to freedom, I chose to experience a range of lifestyles—from poor to rich, socialite to hermit in the mountains—before returning to the Western world I was born into. If you, like me, desire the hermit life yet belong in the city, take comfort in knowing that your home is in your heart even when your heart may not be in your physical home.

Based on my experiences, I would tell any seeker of truth the following: although you may achieve progress on your own, the most conducive environment for personal growth is in the company of others who embody the attitudes and reflect the goals you wish to achieve. Forget the movies, the bars, the hedonistic vacations. Spend every moment of your time with people who are progressing on the path you wish to follow. If those you associate with do not seem to be achieving what you wish to attain, then seek out another group or a teacher. Search the world for these people, look in the most unlikely places, and never give up.

For example, it was only after much searching that I found a Tai Chi teacher at an improbable location in Taiwan—on the roof of an old run-down building in an industrial sector of Taipei. To get to the rooftop, I had to walk up five flights of stairs in a neighborhood that felt so dangerous I wondered if I would get out alive. With each step, I forced myself to continue, because I could not believe I was in the right place; yet up on the roof I found a group of people who were serious about their practice.

Spiritual searching is worth all the effort it takes. Don't rest until you find your home. The home you will be seeking, of course, is not a physical place with a roof and four walls. Rather, the true home is a *state of mind* and a *way of living*.

While locating your path and following it home, remember that nothing is impossible. Even seemingly unalterable circumstances can sometimes change, as is illustrated by the following true story.

When temperatures are very cold, about thirty degrees below zero, it is impossible for snow to fall. However, one winter day in Montreal a few years ago, thermometers were registering forty degrees below zero in the midst of a huge snowstorm. The impossible had happened! What had defied Mother Nature's laws was the presence of a high-level warm air mass above the very cold air mass affecting climatic conditions in that area. The upper-level air mass, as it turned out, was warm enough to produce snow, and the resulting humidity was high enough to propel it through the cold air and onto the ground.

Like the laws of nature, the laws guiding human activity can be broken by the presence of an unusual situation. Similarly, circumstances of life may be rearranged or circumvented to change the expected results. Our capacity to alter limiting or unfavorable circumstances has nothing to do with background, IQ, or social position, but rather with our attitude toward those circumstances and our willingness to exercise creative options and self-control.

This book presents many principles you can use to find your home, temper your attitude, and change the outcome of adverse circumstances. Ultimately, the goal is to stand like a mountain no matter how buffeted you may be by life's changing breezes.

Introduction

From my travels around the world, I learned that a common goal of mystical practices is equanimity—balance of mind. Why equanimity? Because when the mind is at rest, we are open to an experience of the divine. It is in this state that we find eternal contentment, which can significantly improve our personal lives, increasing our financial prospects and leading to more harmonious relationships.

Balance of mind does not eliminate feelings of pain and suffering, but rather lets us know that despite their presence we can experience deep joy and love. It's like mixing the shock of ice cold water with the pain of boiling water—together, they give us the comfort of warm water. When the mind knows that all opposites exist simultaneously, and that there is nothing to fear or try to control since polarity cannot be avoided, it relaxes into its potential for a mystical experience.

The spiritual path presented in this book will take you to a place of balance where opposing feelings coexist and both sides of the emotion scale are equally weighted. From there anything is possible, for it is the cultivation of equanimity that brings about mystical experience, not the other way around. The Sufi tradition defines equanimity as freedom—liberation from all concerns about what others think or say about you. Such a state leads to comfort and contentment, or what we think of as balanced living, the precursor to divine experience.

Practical Mysticism not only points the way to equanimity but also describes how to live by spiritual principles and how to apply them in business transactions as well as social relationships. In effect, it presents an educational system geared to developing the full array of human faculties. Chapter after chapter, you will find ways to become an emotionally and mentally strong, well-balanced, independent individual who no longer acts out of programmed responses to the world. Then the more you open your mind to your unlimited abilities, the more your business and relationship difficulties will dissolve.

Do not expect immediate gratification, however. This is long-term work yielding only subtle results along the way. You may not see how much you've changed until well after the alterations have taken root.

To escape our limitations, we human beings need to understand how *self*-limiting we actually are. Although we are geniuses capable of doing anything we can envision, we are also foolish, for we fail to acknowledge our creative potential and to follow our intuition. We fail at these tasks because we are creatures of habit, and the lazy part of us tends to choose injurious habits. As a result, we often expend tremendous energy conceiving ideas that are destructive to ourselves, other people, and the planet. But it is just as easy to take on habits that promote creativity, freedom, high levels of achievement, and harmony. To move in this direction, we simply need to open our minds to our unlimited potential and recognize how we prevent ourselves from achieving it.

The key to unlocking our potential is to *master our habits rather than allow them to master us*. This means choosing our habits wisely. If instead, we continue to let society, family, or friends select our habits for us, we will continually bump up against our own helplessness. For example, how many times this week have you uttered harmful words as a result of an ingrained tendency to speak before thinking? By repeating our programmed behaviors, we continually limit ourselves, as the following story suggests; however, by choosing our habits, we begin to govern our lives.

One day, a newlywed wife decided to make a special pot roast for her husband. She prepared the meat and, before setting it in the pan to braise, cut off a chunk from each end. When her husband asked why she cut off the ends of the roast, she said she did not know but saw her mother cook roasts that way.

The next day the curious husband went to ask his mother-in-law about the cutting of the roast. She, too, did not know the reason for this practice, and said she did it because her mother always cooked roasts that way.

And so to the grandmother he went. In answer to his question, she replied, "Because long ago when I was young, roasts used to be so big and ovens so small that I had to cut the ends off the meat so it would fit inside."

How can this habitual nature of ours be overcome? By acknowledging its existence and understanding its ways. The exercises, strategies, and stories you will find in the following pages help foster an understanding of our lower nature and of how the mind works. Progressing further, you can then invite your higher nature to emerge as the guiding force in your life. With that comes freedom and true peace of mind.

In addition to understanding, another primary ingredient for moving beyond our habitual nature is willpower—a faculty that helps us maintain our chosen direction in life. Hence in these pages you will also find a method for developing willpower, which is altogether different from the psychic power used to read minds, move objects, and see auras. Psychic phenomena can distract us from our goals, inflating the ego and producing feelings of superiority, which may end up hampering our spiritual growth. Instead, this book focuses on cultivating the highest human faculties, beginning with humility.

Another faculty this book explores is the ability to flow with life—a teaching from the Chinese mystical philosophy of Taoism. From this teaching we learn that if you are in a forest and a tree is falling, you can let it fall on your head and cry out about how cruel God is or you can move out of the way and remark on your good fortune at having been saved. Taoists would say you save yourself by being attentive to what is happening around you, whether you are walking in a forest or making an important business decision in a fancy office.

The New Age movement has turned spirituality into a business, but what is actually needed is to make business more spiritual. This mission, too, forms a central underpinning of *Practical Mysticism*—

not in an esoteric way, but in a thoroughly practical one, by advocating that certain spiritual truths be applied to business operations and personal relationships.

Making business more spiritual has vast ramifications. It has been shown, for example, that improving the lives of employees results in higher productivity and profits—an application of the Golden Rule, "Do unto others as you would have them do unto you." A company reaping these rewards by applying spiritual teachings can in time affect the entire industry by inspiring the competition to implement the same principles. Eventually, leading industrialists may join together to knowingly or unknowingly support human evolution.

As you will see, there are several parts to the Practical Mysticism program, together with dozens of exercises and everyday suggestions. Even if some seem only marginally important to you or reminiscent of strategies you have already tried, approach them all with an open mind, for each one is integral to becoming a practical mystic. It is impossible to say which stone holds up the top block of a pyramid, since they all do the job together.

Questions to Ask Yourself

Before embarking on these teachings, take a moment to answer the following questions. Write out your responses, and refer to them once a month. This will help you determine your goals, monitor your progress, and stay on track.

◆ **What do I really want in life—money, fame, spiritual growth, emotional fulfillment, peace of mind? Which goals consume me the most, and why?**

What you think you want may not be what you really long for deep in your heart. Searching your heart, you are apt to find that whereas money would free you to pursue your interests, it would not satisfy your innermost needs; that the desire for fame may actually be a need for recognition in order to compensate for low self-esteem; that a yearning for spiritual growth, while sincere, may be for purposes of wielding power over others. Consider deeply what you want and your reasons for wanting it.

◆ Am I willing to devote the next five years to achieving my goals?

Five years can seem like a long time, and may not actually be required, but consider the difference it will make to the rest of your life. Thinking long-term will also prepare you to ponder the effect your life may have on the world that your children and theirs will inhabit, or that you yourself may be reborn into.

◆ Why do I live in a situation that is not conducive to achieving my goals? Why don't I make decisions that will lead to the fulfillment of my goals?

Perhaps you have not yet maximized your freedom to choose. This freedom is both a blessing and a curse—it gives you the chance to design your own life and it provides endless opportunities for making self-destructive choices, or opting *not* to choose.

◆ What am I willing to do to achieve personal freedom?

Are you willing to do anything that does not hurt another being? Are you willing to give up everything that no longer serves you? This course of action, although essential, is not easy. Attempting to relinquish something that does not serve you but offers a sense of security is like trying to release the straps of a heavy shopping bag full of goods that you have been carrying for a long time—your hand hurts, yet your fingers can't relax and let go. It takes tremendous strength of character to significantly modify a lifestyle.

◆ How am I supporting my personal growth? What am I doing to accomplish the end results I believe I want?

We think we know ourselves, but what we know of ourselves is an illusion. We know who we *think* we are, who we have been *programmed* to be, but rarely do we know who we were *born* to be. The greatest illusion of all is that we think we want personal growth. To unmask this false front, ask yourself if you are making the best possible choices and taking the necessary actions to achieve your presumed goals.

Good choice-making hinges on leading a conscious life. And a conscious life can be attained only by working on ourselves—by realizing, first of all, that we are asleep and cannot make better choices until we awaken, and by practicing self-observation to help us awaken. Your life and your work is a private matter between you and your god. Despite societal pressures and expectations, you can learn to stay calm and true to your inner visions by focusing on what you do and how you think. The more effort you apply, the better the results will be.

If amassing wealth is your goal, for example, try this exercise while taking a shower or while grappling with a headache or toothache. Ask yourself: "What would be different if I were the richest person in the world?" You would probably have a nicer bathroom, but even if you were emperor of the world you would still be subject to physical needs and pains. A toothache, in other words, hurts just as much if one is rich or poor. Those who are rich may be able to buy drugs to help ease the pain to some degree. Yet all people, no matter how much wealth they have amassed, experience the agonies that accompany the processes of birth, life, and death. This thought can calm the ego and bring grandiose or self-deprecating thoughts into balance.

◆ Who was I before I was born? Who will I be after I die? Who am I really?

Until we know who we are, our willingness to follow directions can give us a clearer picture of our true capacities. That is the purpose of the exercises and instructions set forth in these chapters. If we lift a boat's sail halfway, we will never catch the wind and hold a straight course to our destination. If we unfurl it completely, we will be able to change tack and come about as need be, moving ever closer to our goals.

Explanation of Terms

To gain the most benefit from this book, it is a good idea to have a preliminary understanding of the following terms and concepts.

May these brief definitions help guide you on your journey to becoming a practical mystic.

ASLEEP/AWAKE   States of being along a continuum of consciousness. A premise underlying many Eastern traditions is that we think we are awake but we are actually asleep. We are in a "waking sleep," like a vivid dream, as we drive to work, wash dishes, cook meals, do business, and converse with other people. Because we are not fully conscious of what is going on around us, we cannot function at our optimum level and hence miss many of life's opportunities. To be in control of our lives, we must awaken.

BRAIN AND MIND   Distinct parts of us that govern different aspects of our being. The *brain* is a physical organ that functions mechanically to control body movements. By touching a particular part of the brain, for example, we can cause the hand to move. The brain can even control certain bodily functions, although it is the mind that tells the brain how to proceed.

But where, and what, is the mind? According to Eastern belief, it is located in the center of the chest. Although it is not a physical organ, it rules us—or rather, affects how we rule ourselves. The mind is the part of us that thinks, intuits, interacts with the world, and forms personality traits. To gain command of our lives, it is necessary to control our mind, which we can learn to do through self-discipline. We develop self-discipline by approaching everything we do— whether it is meditating, praying, creating art, walking, talking, or playing golf—with full attentiveness.

The mind is also what differentiates us from animals. And the true nature of mind is what we need to discover as we cultivate equanimity.

CONTEMPLATING   Passively allowing a thought to relax in the mind and letting concepts arise on their own.

FRAGMENTED SELF   The personality with its many little "I's." We think we are one person, but in fact we are fragmented beings convinced that we are unified. Plagued by endless contradictions between what we believe we want and what we actually desire, we constantly rationalize our behavior. We can want to do something (when one I makes a decision to act) and then not do it (when another I with its own agenda takes charge), or vice versa, all the while justifying our actions. Ultimately, there is one central I, our soul, that is the essence of our being. This central I wants to be in charge, but the thousands of little I's vying for control remove it from power, wreaking havoc within us. A major goal ofthis program is to defragment ourselves and become one unified being.

KARMA   An Eastern belief that all actions cause reactions. When we act, there is a reaction; and that reaction triggers another reaction. This endless sequence of cause and effect is called the Wheel of Karma. All actions cause the Wheel of Karma to turn, which is what ties us to this world lifetime after lifetime. Had we not created karma in our past lifetime, we would now be free to live as we wish, based on our true desires rather than on the chain of events we have set in motion. Similarly, the karma we do not complete or correct in *this* lifetime will carry over into the *next* one. To stop creating karma, we must seek out the causative roots of our actions, at which point we come closer to seeing the source of all things, gain control over our habitual behaviors, and replace them with wise actions.

LEVELS OF UNDERSTANDING   The various depths at which a concept may be mastered. The ideas presented in this book, as in life itself, must be understood sequentially if we are to reach new depths of comprehension. If one thought seems to contradict another, recognize that it is simply taking you one step further. Allow your mind to remain open, piecing together portions of the puzzle chapter by chapter before assembling them for the full picture. Since repetition is integral to this process, please accept the apparent redundancies, for they can help deepen your level of understanding.

PERSISTENCE   Perseverance at any task until it is completed, regardless of how long this takes or how much effort it entails. Persistence, the key to success, can be understood by contemplating the story of "The Three Little Pigs," which suggests that the type of "house" we build determines its durability. A quick-and-easy approach to finding our truth is less likely to contribute to the staying power of our inner strength or equanimity. In other words, you cannot read a book or take a weekend workshop and expect to become enlightened or to become a millionaire overnight; the path to self-growth requires daily practice for an entire lifetime at the very least.

PRACTICAL MYSTICISM   A method of learning based on the author's twenty-five years of study and travel in over thirty countries. Practical Mysticism draws from age-old and modern-day Eastern and Western mystical, spiritual, psychological, and physical practices, and explains how they can be implemented in today's world. The practices may be applied to all facets of life, including business, personal finances, relationships, and spiritual development. They are designed to enhance the mind and body as well as the heart and soul—the mortal as well as the immortal parts of our being. When fully implemented, this program promotes the capability to stop living from past programming and to start living consciously, in full charge of our lives, as the creative individuals we are destined to be.

QI GONG (pronounced Chee Gung)   A Chinese physical meditative practice consisting of a series of static postures. Qi Gong is known to improve physical health and mental clarity. To benefit from its many subtle aspects, locate a good qualified teacher rather than trying to learn it from a book.

RESPONSIBILITY   The accountability we hold for our own conduct. Since we are each a product of our actions, we cause much of what happens in our lives. Gifted with freedom of choice, we either determine the course of our lives or accept the programs our parents and society present us with. Since you are liable for your actions and their results, if you perform an act that causes a problem for another person, you are obligated to fix it—at your own expense if need be.

SELF-OBSERVATION   A basic exercise in awakening that entails "watching" what we are thinking or doing at any given moment, as if from the perspective of another person. The purpose of this practice is to gain insight into who we really are, how we think, and how we use our time and energy. Only by knowing yourself can you use your talents to their fullest capacity.

SUCCESS   The accomplishment of a truly desired physical, financial, emotional, or spiritual endeavor. We get what we want by optimally using our personal assets and opportunities for growth. You alone set the level of success you will achieve.

SUFISM   An Islamic mystical tradition dating back about 1,500 years. A Sufi lives in the day-to-day world, with a job and family, yet makes a conscious effort to clear the heart of negative feelings in order to be a good person and do no harm. Through the practice of Zhikr—the repeated recitation of the names and attributes of God— a Sufi strives to achieve union with the divine by establishing a direct, tangible sense of God's presence at every moment.

TAI CHI CH'UAN   A Chinese martial art consisting of a sequence of movements practiced in slow motion. Tai Chi is of great benefit in improving health, increasing energy, and maintaining flexibility while aging. Because it is also an excellent moving meditation, it allows the practitioner to simultaneously have fun, improve physical skills, maintain health, and meditate. To benefit fully from Tai Chi, be sure to seek out a qualified instructor who has a positive attitude and is in good physical and mental health.

TAO TE CHING   A classic work of Chinese wisdom written by Lao-tzu approximately 2,600 years ago. The Tao makes things happen in keeping with natural evolution and devoid of personal feelings. Being conscious and awake allows us to see the changes going on around us and to live in harmony with them. According to Taoist beliefs, God is real yet impersonal, and we are invested with the power and responsibility to cultivate an awareness of God through studying the body, mind, and environment.

THINKING   Actively using the intellect to understand an idea, rather than simply daydreaming.

I. Self-Discovery

Chapter 1

Waking Up

The difference between a normal state of consciousness and enlightenment is that in one we are asleep and in the other we are awake. One day soon after the Buddha became enlightened, he was walking down the street when a group of holy men, recognizing that he was not an ordinary person, asked, "Are you a god?" He replied, "No." They then asked if he was an angel or some other type of spirit, and again he said no. Finally they asked, "So what are you?" And the Buddha replied, "I am awake." Indeed, the word *Buddha* means The Awakened One.

We ordinary mortals are to varying degrees sound asleep. How often do we drive to work and, upon arriving, realize we can't remember a thing we passed along the way? Although our senses have taken in a variety of stimuli, we are left with little awareness of our environment and the events occurring around us.

The state we normally live in is similar to walking down a street, passing within inches of a $100 bill, and failing to notice it. Imagine what it would be like to consciously perceive everything around us. At work, we would get more done without error, which would impress our superiors and clients. In our relationships, we would know what other people are feeling; be able to sense their moods; and respond appropriately, improving communication and goodwill. In our spiritual life, we would be equipped to make developmental choices based on increased self-understanding. So it is that waking up can enhance every aspect of our being.

The first step toward awakening is to realize we are asleep. The next is to recognize that while slumbering we are missing opportunities, restricting the control we have over our lives, and diminishing our potential. There then arises a desire to awaken. The journey to becoming a practical mystic is actually quite simple, for in paying attention to our sleep state we are awakening.

What is it like to be awake? Awake individuals are content and comfortable in any place, at any time—as at ease in a luxurious

palace as in an isolated desert. Approaching every situation with
equanimity, they are free of distractions and able to focus consciously on spiritual evolution. With this comes liberation from limited thinking and from restricted modes of living. Awake individuals
also rely on intuition, the language of the soul. This is the path of the
practical mystic.

Man As Machine

Have you ever spoken to someone who was not registering your
message, only to find yourself getting increasingly angry, just as you
might at a malfunctioning machine? When a machine does not
work, we sometimes hit it or yell at it out of frustration—none of
which does any good since the machine is not conscious and awake.
So it is with people. Most individuals cannot hear what we are
saying. They are as inert as "sleeping" machines, and hence there is
no point in expecting them to understand.

Ultimately, a machine is only as good as its operator. If a driver
falls asleep at the wheel, his vehicle will most likely run off the road.
An aviator can go one step further by operating his craft on automatic pilot; once in the air, he pushes a button, whereupon the
plane, if properly equipped, flies to its destination, enters a landing
pattern, descends, and comes to a nice stop at the end of the runway.
So it is that some people get stuck in a ditch while others run on
automatic pilot, sleeping throughout the entire journey of their lives.
Spiritual quests are conducted in the same ways, as the following
Sufi story illustrates.

*A man named Fazi was searching for the great spiritual guide known as
Khidr. More angel than man, Khidr was easy to recognize because he
glowed with green, the highest spiritual color in the Sufi tradition and one
reflective of truth.*

*One day while on his quest, Fazi was dashing through the streets of a
town when a man asked him, "My son, what are you doing running here
and there?"*

"I am looking for Khidr," Fazi replied.

"How will you know when you find him? Have you ever seen him?" asked the stranger.

"No, I have never seen him, but I have studied hard and am very intelligent and knowledgeable. I will know him when I see him."

The stranger then extended his finger, pointing the way to the next town, and as he did his finger emitted a green glow. Fazi thanked him and ran off in the direction indicated, never realizing who he was talking to.

This story suggests that if you are asleep no amount of knowledge will help you see what is in front of you. It is possible to lead a much more productive and satisfying life by waking up and taking control of your consciousness.

Below is the first in a series of awakening exercises. With regular practice in all four of them, you will become better able to control your consciousness, enhance your perceptions, and respond wisely to events in your world. As a result, your life will change dramatically.

Exercise 1–1

How Awake Am I?

Try paying attention to your right hand for a half hour, maintaining an awareness of every texture, sensation, and air temperature that comes its way. If you are awake, you will be able to sustain this focus without interruption.

Seeing how difficult it is to work with exercise 1–1, you might realize that you are functioning much like a machine and would rather spend your life trying to be permanently awake. Many of us with similar stirrings try to wake up and, believing we are progressing, soon become contented and return to the sleep state; then agitation sets in when we realize we are not making as much progress as we thought. To check on your progress, try exercise 1–2.

Exercise 1–2

How Awake Am I *Now*?

Try to recall ten sights you passed during your most recent drive. Does part of the drive seem like a dream? Are other parts a total blank? How much do you remember of the trees, buildings, pedestrians? How awake were you while driving?

Frustrated and discouraged, many people who reach this point stop striving for wakefulness, forgetting that a true glimpse at our potential occurs only after agitation has spurred us on to further efforts at awakening. As you embark on your journey, please remember that *experiences of being awake become, in themselves, fuel to continue the exercises of awakening.*

The Many Facets of Our Fragmented Self

We think of ourselves as one being, yet this unified vision is far from accurate. There is one central I that serves as the essence of our being, but we also have an indeterminate number of little I's that randomly take turns at controlling our mental and emotional funtions.

For the most part the little I's are so similar to one another that when they alternate control we behave somewhat consistently. But occasionally, a very different I will come to the fore, causing us to say or do something we later regret. For example, when we are faced with a predicament and an I responds according to its tastes and desires, the next moment another I may take over, prompting us to feel differently about the same situation. At such times it seems as if our morals have changed, causing us to act in defiance of an earlier held belief. This confusion in identity is like being in a bar and knowing we shouldn't have another drink yet promptly ordering one anyway.

The fact is that in any segment of time we are accessing the truth of that moment, then an I with another viewpoint responds, presenting us with a different truth. Because each of these little I's is very smart, it can fool us into believing we desire what it alone wants, as if it were our total being.

All these I's make it very difficult to develop to our fullest capacity. One I may say it wants to do this work of awakening, then another I comes along a moment later and wants to go to a movie. One I recognizes that a breakthrough in limited thinking would be of great benefit, while another assumes it would require too much effort to be worthwhile. Such contradictions in our personality impede our path to awakening. Painfully aware of the pull of conflicting desires, we may decide to simply continue deluding ourselves and remain asleep.

Then, too, many times when we think we are following a true desire, we are actually being controlled by a little I instead of the central I. These little I's can keep us chasing our tails in search of so many different hobbies and interests that we never have time to concentrate on pursuits that are of value to our essence. This state of "active laziness"—another emblem of our fragmented self—keeps us too preoccupied to gear up for the work of awakening.

One way to view the predicament posed by fragmentation is to consider that these I's are to our mind what parasites are to our body. Looking at an eyelash through a high-powered microscope, for instance, you would see countless little creatures residing on it. The human body as a whole is host to millions of living creatures that feed off of it and in some instances eventually destroy it. So it is with the many I's living off of the central I. They can create such turmoil within us that we deplete our energy reserves just coping with them all. But once we recognize them and take action to unify our being, we become better able to live a full and healthy life.

With invasive parasites, the cure is elimination. With the little I's, the remedy is awareness and understanding, as is portrayed in the following story of a great Sufi saint.

One day, Ibn Arabi had an overwhelming craving for baklava. Normally he did not like sweets, so he ignored his urge; but it would not go away. When it was time to stop for lunch, Ibn Arabi sat down at a cafe, and before he had a chance to order, the waiter appeared with a plate of baklava, urging him to stop yelling for this thin-pastry dessert. Surprised, the saint stared at the plate before him, whereupon a venomous desert insect crawled out of his nose and ate the baklava, right down to the last drop of honey.

Shocked at the sight of this, the saint glared at the creature that had just come out of him. At that moment, he heard a voice from heaven say, "Now that it has finished eating, put it back in your nose." Which is exactly what Ibn Arabi did.

This story illustrates that the little I's—or in Sufism, the Nafs—are part of the human experience. Unable to be rid of them, we must accept their presence and keep our higher self in charge so that we will not give in to their cravings and demands. But we must never hate the Nafs, for to do so would be to despise a part of ourselves that is simply trying to survive, unaware that it is affecting us. Moreover, to do so would be to reject one of God's creations. Hence instead of hating these venomous pests, we must strive for increased consciousness of them. As it is said in Sufi teachings, "He who knows his Nafs, knows God."

To become more conscious of these fragments of ourselves, we need only watch our shifting opinions and desires, even those that are ever so slight. Then we can begin to seriously do the work of awakening. On days when we do not feel like putting forth the effort, it is best to persist, because each time we force the I in control to do what it does not want to do, it begins to lose strength. Over time, as the I's become weaker, they start to fade like a cloth left out in the sun, at which point our essence, the central I that is our real self, can emerge and take more control of our life. With the central I in charge, we are no longer governed by the law of accident, no longer subjected to the whim of whichever little I is driving us at the moment, and at last free to choose our direction and actions.

Personality, Ego, and Essence

The different layers of our being are the personality, or fragmented self; the ego, intermediary between the personality and our true essence; and essence, or soul, the eternal center of our being. The *personality* layer, as described earlier, contains the many little I's that interact with people and the world, and that compete for power against our essence.

As for the *ego* layer, it consists of a greater ego and a lesser ego. The greater ego, associated with our essence, links our God self to our human self that interacts in this world. The lesser ego, the misguided part that causes us so much trouble, is the portion of our being targeted in teachings that advocate "killing" the ego.

Ordinarily, our every interaction is filtered through the fear- and opinion-ridden lesser ego. Conquering the lesser ego therefore enables our personality to communicate directly with our essence via the unbiased greater ego, helping us interact in ways we were meant to, free of the cloudy filters of fear and subjectivity. At this juncture, we begin to sense what is real in other people.

What are the fears that plague the lesser ego? Essentially, they are worries that the basic human needs for food, shelter, and clothing may not be met. In the clutches of the lesser ego, we wonder: "Who will take care of me when I am old or sick? Where will I live and what will I eat if I have no money?" When the personality is influenced by these fears, it exhibits insecurity, anxiety, and other false character traits rooted in learned behaviors.

Essence is the real, essential self. Overpowered by the fragmented personality, our essence is unable to begin resolving the contradictions between its own desires and those of the little I's. Imaginary and false beliefs sustain the charade. Then when the behavior of the little I's is accepted and understood, the false personality begins to weaken and essence emerges, offering an opportunity for growth. Seen through another lens, we are all part God and part human, yet only when our fragmentation gives way to our central I are we able to realize the God part of us.

We must be careful, however, not to view personality as an enemy to awakening, since it is necessary to have a well-developed personality. In fact, the greater ego's job is to cultivate the personality from a strong essence. The problem is that the lesser ego often intervenes, establishing a personality based on poor programming—

a personality so fragmented that it smothers our essence. At early stages of self-improvement we may think we are bringing out our personality, but we cannot tell if it is arising from our true essence or from learned behaviors.

This work of self-improvement can be compared to the labors of a conscientious gardener who carefully plucks all weeds from his yard. Because the garden of our being has been untended for most of our lives and so many tenacious weeds have taken over, we have a big job ahead of us. Once we have cleaned out most of the overgrowth, though, the work of maintaining a weed-free garden becomes much easier. Our task, then, is to transform our garden of weeds into a beautiful personality nourished by a pure, clean essence.

Whereas the personality is formed from our experiences, essence is the real I we were born with. While the personality conforms to social and cultural conventions, essence is beyond programming and conformity. To find our essence, we have to dig through the personality, much like mining the earth to uncover precious diamonds.

The Work of Awakening

To wake up, we must first see that personality and essence are not one and the same, as we may have believed, but rather two entirely different layers of our being. Our personality was formed by all that we absorbed while growing up. Our essence, beneath it, is what we were born to be. We can untangle the confusion by observing that whereas adults from other countries are different from us, babies adopted from those countries and raised in ours behave much as we do. So it is that while we, too, have become products of the culture we grew up in, beneath this facade we are also something more.

Discovering our true essence is not easy. There is no McDonald's for spiritual growth. Nor can we see who is behind the mask without first lifting it. But upon lifting it, we cannot help but see that we are fragmented. Although it is difficult to acknowledge that we are not in control of our lives, and not who we think we are, only by doing so can we uncover who we really are. To experience your own fragmentation, try exercise 1–3.

Exercise 1–3

Observing the Fragmentation

To gain awareness of inner conflicts caused by fragmentation, watch what happens when you jump from one activity to another, such as leaving an intimate conversation to answer the telephone. Take note of the relative importance of each activity. For example, are you leaping from a significant task to a minor one because you do not want to deal with certain difficulties? Try to give each situation the value and priority it deserves.

Thus, a major difficulty in awakening is finding our true self, which lies hidden beneath our attempts to be someone we are not. Driven by a desire to "fit in," we do what seems acceptable to our society, culture, or group. However, as you may have experienced in the previous exercise, performing a so-called acceptable action, such as answering the phone, may give rise to a feeling that something is wrong. For some people, this discomfort develops into the distinct sensation that their skin is too small. For others, aware that their behavior is inappropriate or silly, the discomfort produces a desire to make things right, whereupon they begin to act more inappropriately and feel even more foolish. Eventually, the snowball of deception becomes so big it crushes all sense of self-confidence.

Having lost trust in ourselves, we experience a deep sadness and become unable to find our inner voice, our intuition, the voice of God within us. In effect, the line of communication with our essence is cut off when sadness creeps in. At such times we often need to reach out for assistance in elevating our mood. It is written in the Talmud that the voice of prophecy would leave King David when he was in a depressed mood, whereupon "he would sing and play on his harp to raise his spirits, and then the holy presence would come back to him." In Kabbalistic sources and in Sufism, too, certain types of music help elevate the spirit to achieve union with the divine.

Another way out from under the snowball of self-delusion is to give up caring about what is right and wrong as defined by social convention. This release can be achieved by examining cultures around the world, noticing how so many behaviors considered right in one country are deemed wrong in another, and then creating our own standards based on inner guidance. Discovering that "right" and "wrong" are relative terms can inspire us to act no longer out of obligation but out of sincerity, all the while gaining greater confidence in ourselves. This will begin the formation of a new snowball—one packed with self-confidence and an open line to intuition.

If you are curious to know just how crushed you may be under a snowball of deception, try exercise 1–4. The results are likely to surprise you.

Exercise 1–4

How Well Do I Know Myself?

To find out how well you know yourself, observe for one full day how often you compromise your moral standards. For example, you may think of yourself as a person of high integrity and honesty who does not lie or steal. But you might find that you tell small lies, stretching the truth once in a while, or exaggerating. Or you might catch yourself pocketing a small item that does not belong to you.

Throughout the day, try to be 100 percent honest and precise about every word that comes out of your mouth. Compare what you say with who you think you are.

Once you are convinced that your personality and essence are separate layers of your being, and that you are neither in control of your life nor the person you think you are, the work of awakening can begin. Start by sitting down and questioning your priorities, the concerns that merit your attention in the face of competing alternatives. If your top-ranking priorities turn out to be what you assume they are, then think again—or rather, contemplate your *real* priorities. When you have uncovered them, take them on as habits and let them relentlessly guide your actions. Now you can sit in the driver's seat of your life with your eyes wide open, taking control of your mind as you would your car.

Chapter 2

Self-Observation

Self-observation means watching ourselves—seeing what is going on around us, what we are participating in, and how we are participating in it. It means observing everything we do as if we were watching an actor from the director's chair. This practice leads to an awareness of our fragmentation, control over the little I's, and an awakening.

Self-observation is also an examination of the present, not the past. When you observe yourself in day-to-day life, you become better integrated and far more efficient. In fact, the more objective you can be, the more likely you are to awaken. Working with this practice is a bit like putting the cart before the horse: to awaken, you do what you would be doing if you *were* awake.

An immediate benefit of self-observation is the chance to actually see yourself in action. Such impartiality cannot happen under ordinary circumstances, when you are closely identified with what is going on. Detached, however, you are apt to notice that you are not in control of your thoughts and actions, that you are contemplating ideas and doing things for unknown reasons, and that you are getting lost in distractions. Exploring the impressions you have been exposing yourself to—which are actually food for your mind— you may then decide to put only thoughts of value in your mind, through seeing, listening, and reading, for example. Too many people let their bodies go through the school of life while they themselves play hooky; hence while detached, you may also see people asleep and running on automatic pilot. If you do, recognize that you yourself may be in this state. Remember, anyone can be a mirror for another.

Through self-observation, we eventually develop control over our emotions, which prevents us from accidentally causing harm to others or saying words we will later regret. While we are asleep, our emotions run wild, like children on a sugar high bouncing off walls. Often we cannot see what is in front of us because we are in such a rage. Being blind with rage is like snow blindness—it will pass in time, yet not until long after the rage has dissipated. And at that point we may experience a second wave of blinding emotion, obstructing our view of the world about us and keeping us asleep. However, as we begin to watch ourselves in action, we wake up and find ways to take charge of our emotions. Once they are under our control, we will see vast improvements in the skills we have honed and in our creative pursuits, such as painting, music, or other artistic endeavors. Using emotions wisely is itself an art that grants us more freedom and mastery over our lives.

Another practical benefit of observing ourselves is that we can hear what people are saying to us and can therefore respond appropriately. For example, if we watch ourselves at work, we can follow up on details suggested by our boss or coworkers, an undertaking that is sure to be welcomed by management. If we listen for the subtle desires of our partner, we can attend to the thoughtful little details that keep a relationship joyous. In short, as observing individuals we become attentive to details, considerate, and conscious of how our actions affect others. As the Dalai Lama has said, "Our purpose in life is to help as many people as we can, but above all, not to hurt anyone."

To begin looking at yourself objectively, work with these two exercises as often as possible. Each time you practice them, you are bound to discover more and more about how your mind works, and you may soon feel a desire to improve your ability to focus.

Exercise 2–1

Developing Self-Observation

While sitting in a cafe or restaurant, observe other people conversing and interacting. Or imagining that you are a stranger, observe yourself conversing and interacting with friends. In either instance, keep an eye out for automatic mannerisms. How much of what is said is original thought, and how much is robotic repetition?

Now contemplate this statement: "A monologue is one person talking to themselves; a dialogue is two people talking to themselves."

Exercise 2–2

Reporting Your Observations

Observe everything you do and report it to yourself. Out loud say, "I am picking up the glass, I am drinking water . . . walking . . . breathing in . . . breathing out." While driving, say, "I see the car in front of me, the house, the pedestrians." As you go about your daily activities, imagine having a blind companion with you who wants to know everything that is going on. As you describe the events of the day, you may realize that you do not normally see everything and that you are not as much in control of your thoughts as you could be. Keep noticing how asleep you are by trying to be awake.

The Four Centers

To have control over how we lead our lives, we must be awake. To awaken, we must see that we are asleep. Understanding how we function helps us recognize when we are asleep, and therefore helps us awaken.

Our functioning is governed by four centers: the instinctive, moving, emotional, and intellectual centers. Each center, other than the instincts, is divided into three sections: the moving, emotional, and intellectual sections. It is important to be able to distinguish between the centers, and between the sections within each one, so that the most appropriate part of us takes charge in each situation.

The *instinctive center* runs the basic functions that are needed to keep the body alive, such as breathing and maintaining the heart-beat. These functions occur automatically, and can be neither halted nor triggered by conscious thought.

The *moving center* operates the body's movements. This fast-acting center governs walking and other physical activities, including reflexive movements. It activates the body more quickly than the mind can. For example, if an animal darts in front of the car, your moving center would signal you to swerve immediately out of its path; but by the time your intellect processed the event and told your body to react, it would be too late to avert a collision.

The *emotional center* governs our experiences of love, affection, fear, and distaste. Actually, it presents us with an entire spectrum of emotions that we cannot describe or explain intellectually but can relate to only through "gut" feelings. Its optimal use is in developing intuition and compassion, both of which are needed in order to communicate with higher levels of our being.

The *intellectual center* calculates and analyzes situations to determine a course of action that will protect us from harm and lead to a successful outcome. When it is not operating in harmony with the emotional center, it may overlook how its directives can hurt others. Its purpose is to help us interact in this world in the most effective way possible.

Generally, one center will attempt to dominate the others. The one that comes to the fore is usually the center most closely related to the person's nature or talents. A poet, for example, will have a dominant emotional center; for a scientist, the intellectual center will reign supreme.

As a result of these domination factors, people will often rely on the wrong center to resolve problems, and thereby respond ineffectively, if not destructively. In the case of an emotional experience, the intellectual center may take charge and, using its emotional section, create an emotional reaction based on an intellectual decision. For instance, two people who are attracted to each other yet fearful of love turning sour may intellectualize to such an extent that they will undermine their chances for a true emotional experience. Calculating numerous possibilities for trouble in the relationship, they may never even get to know each other.

Calamity is also likely when the emotional center inappropriately takes charge of a business venture, due to an emotional attachment to the outcome. Using its intellectual section to arrive at a decision is apt to leave the person incapable of the detachment needed to conduct a wise transaction. For instance, an artist with a strong emotional attachment to her paintings may find that they never sell. In terms of a spiritual experience, a person in momentary union with the divine may suddenly think, "It's happening!" and promptly lose their sense of connection. The intellectual center's emotional section is so wedded to logic that it cannot sustain the feeling of oneness or any other experience that is beyond rational explanation.

Such maladaptive functioning only arises while we are asleep. As we begin to observe which center we are functioning from, we start to wake up. When we are fully awake, the appropriate center automatically takes control of each situation, bringing about the best possible result with no energy wasted in conflict or confusion.

See how much more effective you can be by increasing your awareness of your four centers. You might begin by approaching every interaction with the following questions: "Am I acting from the appropriate center? Do I know what I am doing and why? Are my thoughts and actions aligned with this situation?"

I was once in business with two partners, Peter and John. Peter had little control over his emotions. While under the slightest stress, he would start pacing like a caged animal. Before long, he'd be yelling and cursing uncontrollably, blaming others for his troubles. John, the key person in the company, was sensitive, quiet, and unable to deal with conflict. One day, John called a meeting where he announced that he was tired of the bickering and wanted to quit. I explained that without him, the company would be lost—along with our sizable investment of time and money.

Immediately, Peter jumped up and began to yell profanities at me, just inches from my face. John sat there defeated, his head in his hands, and I calmly waited for the fire to burn down. After about an hour of watching Peter pace as he screamed about how the problems were all my fault, I came up with a plan and managed to get the two to agree to reconfigure the company's management and continue operating. To Peter, I quietly explained that the new formation would benefit him, since he would no longer have to endure the pressure of the working environment and would still maintain his share of ownership and profits. Right away he stopped pacing. "I guess you're right," he said, and settled down.

Functioning from my intellectual center, I had remained

detached enough from both John's threats and Peter's venomous ranting to save the company, together with my investment. And by not allowing my intellectual center to lead from its emotional section while I was being verbally attacked, I was able to achieve a balance that in the end served us all.

The goal of the practical mystic is to function from all centers simultaneously so that the best equipped one will come to the fore at any given moment. We might think of these centers as our children, each of whom wants to take charge but none of whom is equipped for unilateral leadership. Our job as a good parent is to acknowledge them all and get them to play well together—each taking their turn, but not their sibling's.

Levels of Certainty

How can we be sure enough to know the truth of what another person tells us? There are three levels of certainty, each of which calls for an increasing degree of direct experience, as is illustrated by the following scenarios:

1. Knowledge of certainty. We hear about something—a town, for instance. Thus, we have knowledge of it, but since we have never been there we do not yet know the truth about it.

2. Vision of certainty. We set out to go to that town and see it from afar. Having seen the town, we can say for sure that it is there, but we still do not truly know it.

3. Truth of certainty. We enter the town, walk its streets, and talk to the people who live there. Now we know from personal experience that the town is real and what it is actually like.

These three levels of certainty, a Sufi teaching, often came to the rescue in my business ventures. For example, a few months into my real-estate brokerage career, at the age of twenty-one, I became aware that a buyer and a seller will value the same property very differently.

Using this principle, I was able to save many deals that were about to fall apart, one of which involved a fourteen-story office and retail building a client offered to purchase for $22,000,000—a transaction that took nine months to conclude. He would occasionally call me at 1:00 in the morning concerned about some aspect of the deal. I would point out that his worries were based only on what he'd heard from other people; then after a good night's sleep, I would research a lease or other document, and show him the truth, offering a level of certainty that was stronger than gossip.

There I was counseling a man more than twice my age on the biggest deal of his life. He, in turn, was so impressed with my approach to valuing truth over hearsay that he hired me to manage all his property, including the new acquisition, valued at more than $50 million.

The principle that *we cannot know the truth of knowledge acquired secondhand until we have experienced the phenomenon directly* is operative in all domains of life. For example, if you do not practice meditation with effort and devotion, it is nearly impossible to be certain of its value, since the most you can know about it will be based on others' stories of its advantages or on complaints that it is a waste of time. Secondhand information is often wrong, and thirdhand it can be devastating. Only when we have experienced something for *ourselves* do we understand and benefit from it. Hence whenever possible, we must go to the source.

The discipline involved in regularly "entering an unknown town" and "walking its streets" fosters the growth of willpower. With its increased growth, and our continued movement toward the truth of certainty, we begin to change our lives—physically, financially, emotionally, and spiritually. Living from an inner truth then helps us contain the lesser ego, rein in those little I's, and awaken from the limitations imposed by a lifelong slumber.

Observing Our Thoughts

Each thought that passes through the mind is limited in duration. When one thought begins, it has a fixed amount of power that lasts for only a certain period of time before another thought takes over. How often do you immerse yourself in a task only to become suddenly distracted? How many times a day do your thoughts bounce randomly from one subject to another? Without enough willpower to focus your thoughts and keep them flowing in a logical sequence, you may be unable to complete many tasks. Watching the mind at work can go a long way toward regulating it.

If we focus attention on learning how the mind works, we will indeed see that thoughts arise spontaneously and randomly, as is evident in exercise 2–3. We may then observe when one thought is fading, and consciously replace it with a new one that perpetuates the direction its predecessor was moving in. To succeed in the business world, we must be able to focus our thoughts and bring tasks to completion unhampered by diversions; otherwise, we will make mistakes that take time to correct, and the quality of our work will suffer. To enhance our relationships, we need equally strong follow-through or we will be viewed as unreliable and untrustworthy.

Exercise 2–3

The Distracted Mind

To become more conscious of how lost the mind can get, observe a thought you are currently having. Try to follow it back step-by-step to where it originated. Now go even further back to what was passing through your mind before that thought. Evaluate how connected your present thoughts and ideas are to what you were thinking two minutes ago.

Contradictions and Buffers

While observing ourselves, we can see that what we think we believe is not what we really believe. Why did we not notice this discrepancy before? Because consciousness of all the contradictions in our belief system would be difficult to bear. So that we can function without feeling guilt or remorse over our contradictory behavior, the mind has created buffers in our subconscious, and it is these buffers that prevent us from seeing our internal contradictions.

Buffers send out flares that distract us from being aware of acting incompatibly with our beliefs about ourselves. For example, your muscles may become sore enough to prevent you from doing the housework you detest; or you may procrastinate instead of leaving for a meeting that is sure to involve an unpleasant confrontation. The most obvious buffers are the justifications and memory lapses that obliterate our actions from our mind. Caught in a lie, for instance, you may justify your actions or change the topic of conversation to the day's most newsworthy events, rather then see yourself as a liar.

Great amounts of mental energy are expended in hiding our incongruous beliefs from our consciousness. When we observe ourselves acting at variance with our beliefs, guilt and confusion over our behavior consumes even more energy. The point is that whether we are unconscious or conscious of our contradictions, the energy loss is enormous.

To conserve energy and gain personal freedom we need to gradually eliminate these contradictions. From an energy perspective, the vitality used to create buffers for covering up contradictions is vital to our awakening. In terms of freedom, shaking loose the contradictions lets us engage in activities with all our heart, free of guilt or regret.

To become more aware of how your energy is being wasted by conflicting beliefs, search all your desires and actions for contradictions, and point them out to yourself. For example, you may claim you want to improve your health, but you smoke and rationalize this habit by believing you can quit at any time.

If you are asleep, you will not be able to see the contradictions. In this case, one of two things may happen. Either a shock—anything from an unusually jarring comment to the death of a loved one—will jolt you into wakefulness or you will remain cozily asleep behind the buffers, never knowing that you are ruled by a multitude of little I's and uninterested in developing the willpower to defragment yourself. Further compounding the problem, buffers will sometimes attempt to prevent the pain of shock by setting off a distracting series of unfortunate events in order to keep people who are ill-equipped to deal with their contradictions from seeing them and going mad. Hence while they are asleep, they will remain ignorant and perhaps doubly jeopardized; yet upon their awakening, the buffers will be removed one by one as the individuals are better able to deal with their nagging contradictions.

The immediate goal, then, is to see and consciously remove our buffers; the long-term goal is to outgrow the need for them by eliminating the contradictions within us. Self-observation helps us see the buffers at work as well as the contradictions they camouflage. While observing our mental activities, we can catch ourselves changing our mind, as is emphasized in exercise 2–4, or justifying an action. Then we can search for whatever it is we are covering up. The more we stop justifying our actions, the less reason there will be for new buffers to form. Finally, as a result of our increased awareness of fragmentation, the little I's will begin to join together like little soap bubbles, eventually merging into one big bubble—the central I, the essence of our being.

Exercise 2–4

Stalking Those Contradictions

To increase your awareness of contradictory beliefs, notice each time you're feeling a certain way about a situation you recently felt differently about. Record your observations in a notebook and carry it with you at all times. Notice how many times a week you change your opinions and beliefs.

Walls and Filters

Just as we use buffers to keep from seeing our internal contradictions, we also construct walls and filters for protection against harsh external truths. Walls go up on their own, whereas filters are constructed consciously. Beginning at birth, our subconscious sends up emotional walls to shield us from the pain of seeing our loving parents fight or lie. Initially, these barriers go up and down as needed; later, they go up and stay up. There they remain until they deteriorate and, like any quickly built structure, fall to the ground. Later, when similar events trigger the need for walls, new ones are put up amid the debris. Eventually, it becomes difficult to access our intuition, trapped as it is under these large piles of rubble.

Our subconscious constructs the new walls to protect us from realities we cannot face in adulthood. For example, if we are living with someone who is perpetually negative minded and we are lacking the strength to handle it, barriers go up to prevent us from fully experiencing its effects, thereby creating a more livable situation. Of course, although we will not hear the negativity, the words will still register in our subconscious.

Instead of new walls, which are impermeable, we may decide to assemble an occasional filter, letting in some of the offending content. When we begin to use filters in lieu of walls, the piles of rubble start to dwindle—just as a riverbed erodes beneath a flowing stream that carries no new material into it. The current that carries away the emotional debris is our willingness to look objectively and courageously through filters.

Another advantage of filters is that since we can consciously install them we can consciously remove them. In fact, the more skilled we are in self-observation, the better able we will be to remove them. Then with further awakening, filters will no longer be needed either.

Overcoming Limitations

Self-observation is a profound practice. It can help you see that you are composed of many little I's all vying for control. Once you have acknowledged this fragmented state of being, you can begin to assert control over the little I's. You can also learn how to eliminate buffers and wash away the remains of emotional walls. Then you can start to choose who you are going to be—or better yet, discover who you *really are*. Once you are firmly established on the path to becoming a nonfragmented being, you will no longer need the masks that have been controlling you, and in their place you can consciously put on different masks when you wish to.

Just as there are many I's, so are there innumerable masks representing various facets of our being, which we wear while interacting with others. Normally we function from a single aspect of ourselves at a time, wearing only one of our many masks. This mode of interaction can be terribly limiting. For example, while we are being a teacher to our child, she may also need a compassionate parent, but trapped in our singleness of vision we will be unable to see the necessity for a second mask.

We humans often approach situations from the viewpoint of what we have already learned, rather than thinking creatively about them, as if seeing them for the first time. For example, if someone were to propose the notion of selfless giving and suggest that you offer your services with no expectation of reward, you might reply that you wouldn't be able to make a living that way. Such a response reflects thinking *horizontally,* in a limited manner. If instead you thought *vertically,* with an expanded perspective, you might realize that you could charge clients who can afford your services, yet be of service to others free of charge—for instance, by helping an elderly woman carry her shopping bags, or listening to a teenager in need of a sympathetic ear, or volunteering at the local soup kitchen or homeless shelter.

If we could function vertically—wearing all our masks simultaneously—we would see a situation from several viewpoints at once and, drawing on all the abilities we possess, address it in the best way possible. Vertical thinking is an excellent tool not only for seeing the multifaceted reality of situations but also for creative problemsolving. Whereas many highly specialized people often do not think beyond the confines of their sphere of expertise, by letting our mind expand to take in the entire landscape of possibilities, we can extend our thinking far beyond learned material. In fact, we become open to *everything*.

If we could function vertically, wearing all our masks at once, we would be able to adjust our words and actions to suit any situation. We would then be certain to speak and act wisely. Such a scenario would be all the more profound if we donned the following seven masks:

> Highest consciousness/Spirit
> Normal, everyday consciousness
> Mother/Father /Brother/Sister
> Teacher
> Student
> Worldly necessities
> Animal/Instinct

As you contemplate this totem pole of functions, observe the understanding of it that begins to form in your imagination. Then remind yourself that thinking vertically implies being open-minded and entertaining all possibilities simultaneously, in contrast to being close-minded and maintaining a narrow viewpoint. Can you see that with practice there would be no separation of masks— just one well-rounded, versatile person?

Vertical functioning came to my rescue many times in the construction business when I had to deal simultaneously with laborers determined to be simple folks and investors worth hundreds of millions of dollars. Whereas the construction workers often wanted to have fun with their friends and work at their own pace, the venture capitalists expected to have their desires materialized in an instant. I was often maneuvering between the two, commiserating with the plight of the laborers and encouraging them to work harder while helping investors see that the job was getting done. As a result, the projects were completed on time, if not ahead of schedule, and to everyone's satisfaction. Author Rudyard Kipling referred to this aspect of human potential when, in his poem entitled "If," he wrote about how enriching it is to be able to "walk with Kings" yet not "lose the common touch" (see epilogue).

In addition to helping us speak and act with more wisdom, thinking vertically inspires us to appreciate differences without judging them as superior and inferior. For example, Westerners say it is disgusting to eat insects, while Asians consider them a delicacy; both regard the other's predilection as strange. Rather than view our culture's preferences as superior, it is more broadening and growth promoting to open ourselves to *all* possibilities. This expanded state of consciousness can be approached by remembering first, that we do not know what is real or right, and second, that in overcoming limitations we become more of who we really are—a giant step forward that can be accomplished with the aid of the following exercise.

Exercise 2-5

Moving beyond Stereotypes

To become more of who you are, consider how people of every culture reflect particular beliefs and traditions in their style of clothing, music, and other means of self-expression. Now observe how you perpetuate the stereotype of your own culture. To what degree are you your true self, and to what degree do your likes, dislikes, and dreams for the future merely reflect family and societal expectations?

Chapter 3

Changing Old Habits

We spend our lives trying to reduce suffering and increase physical, emotional, and mental pleasure. When pleasure arises, we accept and enjoy it; when difficulty crops up, we try to cover it over with pleasurable distractions. However, increasing pleasure to alleviate pain is not a lasting solution, since delights that numb suffering are not experienced as sources of true joy. To reach a state of peace, we add layers of these temporary pleasures on top of layers of pain, yet each time we do this we end up moving further *away* from our essence, as is illustrated in the diagram below:

```
——————————————pleasure——————————
——————————— pain——————————
——————————————pleasure——————————
——————————— pain——————————
——————————————pleasure——————————
——————————— pain——————————
——————————— ESSENCE——————————
```

Seeking pleasurable distractions to alleviate pain is doubly self-defeating, for it not only moves us further away from our essence but also increases the obstacles we must contend with before achieving a permanent state of peace. It is only by *eliminating* the pleasure-pain layers that we can tap into our essence, where true joy resides. This does not mean we should refrain from seeking pleasure, but rather that by seeking pleasure to *cover up pain* we are giving ourselves a great deal of work to do.

We can begin to eliminate pain through the practice of self-observation. First we observe the pain; then we disarm the lesser ego. This negative-minded ego has us believing that everything bad in our world is connected to us, giving rise to such remarks as, "If I plan a picnic for this weekend, of course it will rain." By climbing out of our self-pity long enough to take note of these assertions, we will realize we are *not* the cause of everything bad that happens to us, at which point our lesser ego will no longer want to add more layers of pleasure to cover our pain. When a blizzard stops and the sun comes out, it melts the snow on the ground. So it is that the sooner we shed light on our mounds of pleasure-pain and stop contributing to them, the easier it is for the existing ones to finally dissipate.

As the memory of a painful event fades away, so does our recall of who we were when we experienced it. It's almost as if we didn't exist then, and we may remark, "I can't believe that really happened!" At such times we recognize that now we are *here*, living each day of a real life—provided that we are awake to it. If we are asleep, then who we are *now* vanishes along with the memory of the past event.

Seeking to increase pleasure to cover up pain is nothing more than a habit. We are creatures of habit and rarely engage in independent, conscious thinking. Moreover, our lesser egos take life very seriously, weighing us down through the folly of their habitual ways. Although it is possible to stay lighthearted and playful, such an attitude requires a strong, well-developed mind. For this, we must form *new* habits, which takes time and concentrated effort. Seeds for new habits spring from the old ones—in this case, from seeing the absurdity of taking everything so seriously and personally, learning to view life objectively, refusing to seek pleasure as an anesthetic against pain, and above all, remembering that pain is a temporary state. Ultimately, nothing in this world is everlasting, as is conveyed in the following anecdote.

There was once a king who asked his advisers to think of a short phrase he could inscribe on his ring to elevate his mood when he felt depressed yet keep him from getting carried away when life was going very well. One counselor finally came up with the phrase "This, too, shall pass."

Perceptions

If we spend our life pursuing pleasure to alleviate pain, as is the tendency of the mind, we will never be permanently at peace. Why?

Because what comes is what comes, rain or shine. That is the way of the Tao. What matters is how we *perceive* what happens, as this Taoist story illustrates.

A man and his only son worked on a farm with just a single horse to pull the plow. One day, the horse ran away. "How terrible," said the neighbors in sympathy. "What bad luck."

The farmer replied, "Who knows whether it is bad luck or good luck."

A week later, the horse returned leading five wild mares into the barn. "What wonderful luck!" exclaimed the neighbors.

"Good luck? Bad luck? Who knows," answered the old man.

The next day, the son fell and broke his leg while trying to tame one of the wild horses. "How terrible. What bad luck!" said the neighbors.

"Bad luck? Good luck? Who knows," replied the farmer.

Later in the week, a war broke out near the border, and since the local troops were badly outnumbered by the enemy, the army came to the surrounding villages to conscript all the young men into battle. Because of his broken leg, the farmer's son was spared.

Good luck? Bad luck? You never know!

Things simply happen. The winds of life are constantly changing, and what seems fortunate today may appear regrettable tomorrow, or vice versa. Whether an incident results in a positive or negative outcome depends on an entire sequence of events that transpire over time—often a very long time. Understanding that we lack the capacity to see every link on these chains of events can take the sting out of many seemingly bad experiences, freeing the mind to patiently find a benefit in any situation.

One of our strangest quirks is to seek out pain so we can feel pleasure when the agony subsides. This, too, compromises our freedom of mind, for it keeps us engaging in stressful situations to experience the exultation that follows. When we participate in contact sports or other perilous activities, for instance, our adrenaline builds up and is then released as we reach safety, resulting in a high that binds us to stressful situations.

Are you ready to change your habitual views of life? If so, try exercise 3–1. It will show you that you can break free of self-defeating routines and begin to blaze trails to a state of enduring joy. After mastering this exercise, you may want to develop an entire repertoire of positive new habits.

Exercise 3-1

Turn Your Mind into an Alarm Clock

Suppose you are accustomed to setting your alarm for 7:00 in the morning and getting up ten minutes after it goes off. Before falling asleep tonight, repeat a few times, "My mind will wake me up at seven o'clock." First, however, set your alarm for 7:10 as a backup, to ease your mind. Repeat this exercise until you are able to wake up on your own before the irritating sound of your alarm.

Behavioral Habits

Newborns have a blank mind that takes in all sensory impressions without discriminating between good ones and bad. By middle childhood, they have naturally picked up many undesirable habits from their parents, who picked them up from *their* parents. As a young child, for example, I would often hear my father say, "If you can get a job, grab it no matter what it is or what it pays. Stick with it for the rest of your life, and be grateful you have it." Old enough to realize that following this advice would all but guarantee me a miserable existence, I rejected it before it became instilled in me. Many of us settle for handed-down mediocrity because we think it is our lot in life, but our true destiny in this world is determined by either unconsciously accepting an inherited program or writing our own script. In either instance, we are the responsible party.

Because parental habits and attitudes are ingrained in us so early in life, we grow up believing they are ours. Then at some point confusion or alienation sets in, leaving us baffled as to why we feel perplexed or lost while having everything we seemingly want.

The truth is that if we had everything we wanted we would be perfectly content.

This is the time for facing up to the fact that what you think you want is what you have been taught will work, not what your essence knows to be true. Now you must find your true desires. Ask yourself: "Am I as mentally strong as I think I am? Is my mind as free from worry as I think it is? Am I as capable and successful as I think I am?" If the answer to any of these questions is no, begin writing your own script. As an old Chinese saying goes, "It is only through reforming ourselves, not the world, that we can make any practical improvement."

Writing your own script means finding the origins of everything you understand about yourself—every belief, habit, and character trait that forms your personality. Also look at your accomplishments and determine whether they are an aid or a detriment to your growth. While conducting this review, try to observe yourself as an unbiased judge would, and one by one eliminate the scripts that are not yours. By emptying your mind of preconceived notions about yourself, you will regain the perspective of a newborn child whose mind is untainted. From there you can begin to learn who you really are, and behave accordingly. A technique for reevaluating your character traits is described in exercise 3–2.

Exercise 3–2

Uncovering the Real You

To learn who you really are, examine each of your character traits to see if it is something you appreciate or would prefer to change. Claim as your own those traits you value, and discard the rest. Be sure to repeat this exercise periodically, because in response to your examination injurious habits that have been inactive or covert may resurface.

Do you sometimes say with regret, "If I knew then what I know now"? The good news is that there is no need for regret because after practicing exercise 3–2 you will have the power to *return* to "then" with the knowledge you have *now*. In addition, because you have repeated a habitual behavior for ten years and now realize how destructive it is means that you are liberated from having to repeat it for the *next* ten years! As for the traits you have opted to keep, they are not likely to plague you, since their presence is now based on a mature decision. In effect, what you are doing is leaving the past to yesterday and beginning anew today. Although it takes time and effort to discover who you really are, the rewards far outweigh the investment, granting you invaluable information for the future.

Many people are scared to take risks, choosing to play it safe by doing what they were taught as children rather than experiencing life for themselves. But if we want everything life has to offer, we must take risks and live by our own ideas rather than those of others. People who have the courage to make new decisions and take responsibility for their actions are the ones who receive all the riches the universe has to offer and who help build a better world. As Jawaharlal Nehru, India's first prime minister, said, "The success of a thousand men comes to those who dare and act."

Thinking Habits

The East Indian philosopher J. Krishnamurti pointed out that we are bound to a circle of thinking that limits our growth. At birth, we are completely receptive to our experiences, accumulating knowledge from them that we store in our memory. Faced with a new event, we search our memory for a similar one, and react comparably. That reaction causes another event, whereupon we again search our memory for a way to react. And so the cycle is repeated: event, memory recall, reaction, memory storage. In effect, we are like robots, perpetually reenacting the past when the situations facing us are entirely new.

We think we think, but do we really have any original thoughts? When we believe we have formed a thought of our own, we discover its source in something we have either heard or seen earlier in life. To see how trapped you are in a circle of thinking, try the following exercise.

Exercise 3–3

Your Circle of Thinking

Select any thought that comes to mind, then trace it back to its origin. Now trace that thought back as well. See if your mind can come up with a thought that is unconnected to an earlier one.

Similarly, are the opinions you voice spontaneous reflections of your true beliefs or are they based on information you have previously received? Ask yourself if you are really thinking on your own or if you are back in school trying to give the answers your teacher wants to hear. Then next time your opinion is solicited, before speaking take a moment to think about what you want to say, and look for the source of that thought. Is it *your* opinion or does it come from somewhere else? For assistance in this practice, try exercise 3–4.

Exercise 3-4

Thinking about Thinking

To reinforce your ability to trace thoughts to their source and learn to think for yourself, visualize a forest, then focus on a tree, then a branch, then a leaf, and finally a vein in the leaf. Follow that vein through the leaf, back through the branch, inside the tree, down through the trunk, to the roots, and into the earth. From within the earth, which feeds the tree, think of where else you might go. Do this very slowly so that your mind can hold the thread of the visualization.

Exercise 3–4 will help free you from the circle of programmed thinking that limits your growth. It will also help you develop the ability to see beneath the surface level that normally guides human activity.

Another thinking habit that limits our growth is our tendency to operate from a negative frame of mind. The mind, as we have seen, instinctively feeds on impressions; these create the thought forms that influence our frame of mind. Our frame of mind, in turn, determines our financial and personal success, as well as our physical well-being, emotional growth, and spiritual evolution.

To eliminate fear and doubt, the greatest obstacles to success, we must be constantly on guard against negative thoughts that attack from within, and learn to replace them with positive thoughts. For example, if you think, "I will never start a business of my own. How can I make enough money at anything I love to do?" observe the thought and then say, "Oh really? If I try hard enough and open my mind, I can. Go away, negative thought." Speak to each negative thought as if it were a person, and tell it to leave you alone. Explain that you are too busy to pay attention to negativity because you are on your way to success. Another technique for defusing the power of negativity is described in exercise 3–5.

Exercise 3-5

Fending Off Negative Thoughts

To enhance your chances of achieving success, when you catch a negative thought disrupting your mind, think of a person who inspires you. Visualize their face and imagine them by your side. Then allow their strength of character to repel the negative thought until it is gone and you feel calm.

External impressions fed to the mind influence our physical health in equally profound ways. If we are less careful about what we put in our mind than what we put in our mouth, we will defile the body far more than we do by eating junk food. When we immerse the mind in an environment infused with fear and violence, for instance, our body will tense up, restricting blood flow to the organs and interfering with their optimal functioning. People who practice yoga or Tai Chi develop an ability to feel this happening.

The morsels we feed our mind also have an immediate impact on our spiritual growth. In fact, we advance spiritually not so much through good work as through lessening the destructive impressions absorbed by the mind. If we spend days in meditation to bring our mind to a more peaceful state and then watch a horror movie, we will instantaneously undo the good we achieved. To guard against such reversals, spiritual teachings from around the world advise us to spend time each day reading passages from the Bible or Talmud, the Koran, Upanishads, Bhagavad Gita, or any other inspiring text.

Actually, to enhance our prospects for success, good health, and spiritual development, we need to supply the mind with uplifting thoughts and images *daily*. Self-observation and reduced exposure to negative impressions increase our inner peace, yet when we are not deliberately putting positive thoughts into our mind, it will be fed through thought forms floating around in the environment, which are frequently negative, such as those from TV, radio, or gossip. For this reason it is important to read uplifting books rather than submerge yourself in mindless entertainment; to avoid exposing yourself to negative news; and to steer clear of negative-minded people. Whenever possible, also practice the following exercise.

Exercise 3–6

Heightening Your Awareness of Negativity

To increase your awareness of negative influences, examine what people around you say and what you say. Observe the negativity that comes to expression in everyday rhetoric, including colloquialisms and anded remarks. Identify the negative thoughts and expressions that are permeating your life, and one by one weed them out of your mind.

Avoid brushing anything off as harmless. For example, the statement "The traffic is going to be a mess," although commonly uttered, is extremely negative. The traffic is what it is.

In my early twenties I could see that the voice of media so sensationalized negative news stories that people were reacting to them much as they would to a drug. As a result, I stopped reading the newspaper, listening to the radio, and watching TV. Within a few months my outlook had brightened considerably, and I was feeling calmer. Even friends commented on the change in my disposition. As for my knowledge of world events, the news I needed to know still found its way to me from people who loved to talk.

By deliberately feeding your mind positive, inspirational thoughts and staying away from anything that is not an impetus to higher existence, you, too, will notice a profound change. If you already consider yourself a happy person free of negativity, filtering your sensory impressions will result in an increasingly positive and peaceful frame of mind. In either case, to help further eradicate negative thinking habits, note the changes you observe each step of the way. Keeping a journal, such as the one described below, will reinforce your efforts.

Exercise 3–7

Journal of Changes

Purchase a blank book and title it Journal of Changes. *Use it exclusively for recording the changes you have noticed within yourself from the time you started practicing these exercises. Every few days write down differences you have observed in how people are treating you, and how previously troublesome situations or relationships are unfolding—any little miracle that has come your way. Let your journal function both as a witness to the subtle changes taking place and as encouragement to persist when progress seems lacking.*

Paying Attention

When we rid ourselves of thoughts programmed by others, and carefully screen all new thoughts entering our mind, our inner vision clears and we become more balanced. Accomplishing our goals then brings us increased peace because our purpose is being fulfilled. As peace and balance become securely rooted within us, a self-guiding power emerges.

Moving in this direction involves paying attention as much as possible to what we do and say every moment of every day. Once we have overcome our worst habit of all—sleeping with our eyes open—we will be prepared to respond to the opportunities around us. The following story emphasizes the value of such a quest.

A man once heard that a great sage had three secrets for achieving enlightenment. One day after years of searching, he found the sage and begged him to reveal the secrets. "I'll do so," the wise man agreed, "but to guarantee success you must follow them to the letter."

"Of course I will," replied the man, eager to enter into the sublime state.

The sage nodded and said, "The first secret is to pay attention. The second secret is to pay attention. And the third secret is . . . to pay attention."

While paying attention, we become equipped to take advantage of opportunities that arise. Otherwise, miracles and good fortune may pass us by. Miracles, after all, are not always as obvious as the parting of the Red Sea; often they are subtle hints of potential. By awaiting an ideal situation for achieving our goals and overlooking the finer nuances in our midst, we may fail to recognize a not-quite-perfect opportunity that merely needs a bit of work—an opportunity whose potential will develop in due course. Such miracles are challenging to spot since the object of our desire is often obscured in the darkness of sleep.

Hence the practical mystic strives to keep eyes, ears, and most importantly, the mind wide open at all times. The reason for such vigilance is illustrated in this story.

A man was walking on the beach when an officer from the Coast Guard drove up in a Jeep and said, "Get in. A flash flood is coming."

The man replied, "I have faith in God to save and protect me. Go rescue some unbeliever—I'll be fine."

The floodwaters came in. When they were up to the man's waist, Coast Guard officers arrived in a raft to save him, but he sent them away with the same reply. The water rose to his neck, whereupon several men in a boat came to save him. He sent them away as well, professing his belief in God's protection of the faithful. Finally, the water rose so high that the man drowned.

When he met God, the dead man was confused and angry. "All my life I was a good man and believed in you and your teachings. I had faith that those who believed in you would be protected. Why did you not save me?"

God replied, "My son, I sent a Jeep, a raft, and finally a boat. What more did you want?"

Daily Practices

Discarding old habits, choosing new ones, and paying attention to opportunities for growth takes ongoing work. To support you in your efforts, here are several practices to incorporate into your day. The first two are best performed soon after opening your eyes in the morning.

◆ **Increase and maintain your flexibility.** For an alert body, do the following stretching exercises gently, preferably while still sitting in bed. That way your body will be warm, and your muscles relaxed enough to stretch easily. With each hand, foot, and head movement, hold the stretch for about five seconds, then slowly release it.

First, stretch the joint of each finger for a few seconds, bending it backward. Then move on to the whole hand, bending it back and forth to stretch the wrist. Next, hold your forearm and rotate the wrist in each direction about five times. Repeat this sequence with your toes and feet.

Slowly turn your head to the left, looking behind you as far as you comfortably can without moving your shoulders or torso, then to the right, then back to center. Now touch your chin to your chest. Tilt your head as far back as possible. Finally, returning your head to an upright position, try to touch your left ear to your left shoulder, then your right ear to your right shoulder. Repeat each movement three times.

This stretch is for the eye muscles, so if you are wearing glasses, please remove them. Without moving your head, look as far as possible to each side, holding for two seconds; now look up, then down, then diagonally to either corner for two seconds each. Repeat these movements three times. When you have finished, rotate your eyes full circle about five times in each direction.

◆ **Write notes to yourself,** saying, "Watch the negative thoughts." Place these notes wherever you are likely to see them, such as on the bathroom mirror, on the refrigerator, near your desk, and on the steering wheel of your car.

The next six practices will help boost your energy level as the day progresses. Note any changes you observe and record them in your journal of changes.

◆ **Build self-esteem and confidence** by frequently saying to yourself, "I am capable of accomplishing any job I choose to do." Watch out for conflicting thoughts and eliminate all negative ones, such as "Someone with my background could never achieve the level of success I desire."

◆ **Slow down your physical movements** and pay attention to each move you make. You may be surprised to discover that moving slowly will not stop you from getting things done quickly. Not only that, but in combination with paying attention, it will help you make fewer mistakes and thus be more efficient.

◆ **Change your eating habits.** Eliminate an unhealthy food or ingredient from your diet and, if you like, replace it with something new. Altering your eating routine in this way can increase your energy level.

◆ **Change another habit** by replacing it with something new. Some people are able to quit smoking or drinking all at once, provided that they have sufficient willpower to take on the challenge. Controlling your habits, whatever they may be, will stop them from controlling you.

◆ **Take a new route to work.** Along the way, pay attention to the houses, the people, the trees, the sky. While driving, each time you stop at a red light, look at the passengers in the vehicle next to you; take note of any blank expressions and ask yourself if *you* want to look like that. While walking, say hello to people you pass on the street; observe their reactions.

◆ **Pay attention** to yourself and your environment. The more aware you are, the better prepared you will be to welcome new and exciting opportunities that may help you succeed.

There is a Chinese saying that "a journey of a thousand miles begins with one step." So does the journey toward self-discovery. With each subsequent step, you will be setting foot on new ground. Every corner you turn will give you a fresh sense of direction. You are the guide on this trek. And it is one that only you can take, for it leads to the core of your being.

II. The Worldly Side of Life

Chapter 4

How to Succeed

Regardless of how much we have learned about ourselves, self-discovery alone cannot lead us to equanimity. Why? Because we do not live in a vacuum. To continue progressing toward a balanced state of mind, we must take into account the worldly side of life—its observable pushes and pulls as well as its more subtle dynamics. How we interact with the material world will in large measure determine the degree to which we will prevail in our quest. The opposite is also true: the more balanced and peaceful we become in our personal lives, the more success we will enjoy in our worldly pursuits.

Society tells us that if we do not achieve our goals it is because we are not trying hard enough, and that working more diligently is the only way to increase our chances of success. This message has been passed down throughout time. However, it is not entirely true.

Certainly, work is required to achieve any goal and some goals require more of it than others, but the real key to success is the reduction and eventual elimination of negative actions, thoughts, and emotions from our lives. Reducing wind drag on its own increases the speed of any vehicle, and the same principle applies to acquiring money, fame, inner power, or peace of mind.

Motivation

Motivation figures prominently in the success we will achieve and in how satisfied we will be with the results of our endeavors. In fact, results are often connected more to motivation than to the actions undertaken.

For example, when I was young, my parents often complained about not having enough money. Although my father worked very hard, there was always something they wished they could do if only they had more funds. When I was thirteen, they took me to the annual automobile show in Montreal. Seeing a strawberry red convertible at the Mercedes display, my mother, who did not drive, said she would learn to if she had a car like that. My love for my mother was so strong that I promised I would buy her a Mercedes one day. This motivating force fueled a determination to start my first business soon afterward. Ten years later I purchased a Mercedes. She still would not drive, so I used it myself, yet the motivation to please my mother is what led to the purchase.

But what if after achieving our goal we find it does not provide the expected satisfaction? The problem may be that our motivation was not what we thought it was. Suppose you want to make enough money to buy a boat, yet on a subconscious level your motivation is not to have a boat but to prove yourself to your father or to show off to friends out of an inner need to bolster your self-worth. Since your true motivation is at odds with your perceived motivation, the boat may not offer the satisfaction you had hoped for, or you may not even acquire the funds to buy it.

Most of us do not know why we act as we do, but with a little effort the real reasons eventually become clear. To find out why you choose the goals you do, periodically question the apparent motivation behind your efforts, asking yourself, "Do I really want this particular object (outcome)?" If the answer is no, ask, "Then why do I seem to want it?" Next, ask yourself, "What object (outcome) do I actually want, and why do I want it?" In unearthing the true motivation behind your actions, you will tap into a huge wellspring of power. And because of your honesty, your work will produce increasingly rapid and desirable results.

One man I know became a lawyer but grew to hate the profession. Within three years of starting his legal practice, he fell ill and ended up in the hospital, taking six months off from work to recuperate. While recovering, he pursued his hobby of photography and, realizing he had become a lawyer to please his family, decided to embark on a career he could enjoy. As a result, he left his law practice and began making his living as a photographer, which he has been doing now for thirty happy and healthy years.

Other people I know would like to turn a cherished hobby into a profession but the lazy parts of their fragmented self convince them that the effort involved would be too overwhelming, the task too difficult, and the income insufficient; consequently, their hobbies remain pastimes. This is especially true of men and women whose childhood enthusiasm was disregarded and whose dreams were squelched as mere "fantasies" or "whims." By their late teens or early twenties, many of these people received the message that life is difficult and success impossible, especially if they were to follow their "foolish" dreams. As a result, the fire of their enthusiasm died; and no longer motivated to succeed, they gave up on their destined path of work. During adulthood, experiences of this sort tend to show up as generalized apathy and a humdrum existence.

If you are a parent, be sure to support your children's desires, even if they are short-lived, rather than pouring a big bucket of you-can't-possibly-do-it or we-can't-afford-it cold water over their heads. Let their enthusiasm excite you, and try to remember what it was like for you to be motivated by dreams. If funds are limited, help your children find a cost-effective approach to pursuing their dreams.

From motivation comes action—a train powered by the steam of determination. The fire of enthusiasm and motivation boils the water of creative ideas, producing the steam that turns a concept into a reality. We cannot get enough steam to move into action without a big hot fire of enthusiasm, and what keeps this enthusiasm alive is effort and persistence.

To appreciate the role played by effort and persistence, imagine that you are stranded in the wilderness and must build a fire to keep warm. Having no matches, you find two sticks and begin rubbing them together, noticing that producing enough friction to ignite a spark takes *effort*. Any time you stop producing friction, the heat that has built up will quickly dissipate, forcing you to start over again, and hence you must have *persistence*. When with effort and persistence you finally manage to start a fire, you will no doubt feel enthusiastic about your accomplishment—all the more so since it will help you survive the night and allow you to continue on your way in the morning. With this in mind, imagine what it would feel like to fuel an idea that may change your life.

Often you will find that the only noticeable difference between people who are very successful and those who are not is that the former have great fire because they never give up. If they are involved in a project that fails, they look at what they could have done better rather than give up or point the finger of failure at someone else. If the failure was beyond their control, they seek out ways to have more control over the next attempt, which may also entail more control over themselves. Successful people do not blame others or external circumstances, and do not dwell on things that go wrong. Instead, they stoke up a roaring fire of enthusiasm and motivation, and embark on a new attempt to achieve their goals.

If you have failed in the past, you may need to reignite your fire of motivation. To begin, try to remember what it felt like to be really motivated—to eat, sleep, and even breathe with a goal in mind. Then pick a direction that feels right to you, putting all your effort into it for six months to a year, regardless of whether the interim results are encouraging. If your former occupation was not satisfying, look for an endeavor that holds possibilities for success and satisfaction. Remember to remain committed to your growth and freedom through devotion to your goal. But be careful not to get involved with get-rich-quick schemes or fast-and-easy enlightenment programs, since such endeavors tend to bring about unfavorable results. Long-term success takes long-term effort, not just luck. As a practical mystic would say, "I'm a firm believer in luck. The harder I work, the luckier I get."

Focusing Energy

To fire up our motivation, we simply need to focus our energy on a task we would like to complete. If we delve into too many projects at once, however, we may never complete any of them. Imagine sitting in front of a large woodpile and feeding one log at a time to a fire, as opposed to trying to feed one hundred fires. With only one fire to feed from the woodpile, you'd be able to keep it burning hot and strong. With one hundred fires, you'd be running from one blaze to the next, spreading the fuel too thin to keep any of them going, and your efforts would result in cinders.

The meditative practice of focusing energy on a single task enhances our sensitivity and awareness as we awaken. If we persist without distraction or discouragement, the fire of motivation will ignite—or be rekindled—and we will succeed at our task.

That is what happened to me when, at age twenty, I decided to become a real estate agent. The training course would last eight weeks, I was told, and the next program was to start in about a month. Since I did not want to wait three to four months for a license and since the final exam for the current program was only three weeks away, I asked if I could buy the books, study on my own, and sign up for that exam. Permission was granted, although dubiously.

Each day after finishing my full-time job, I would spend the evening studying. I read the course manual for three weeks, usually until 2:00 or 3:00 in the morning, waking up again at 7:00 for my job. Despite this hectic schedule, I remained motivated, because real estate had long excited me. As it turned out, I topped the 40 percent failure rate on the test, scoring 96 percent—most likely because the majority of candidates were merely trying to get a job to feed themselves whereas I wanted to change my world.

Real estate brokers claim that 10 percent of the agents make 90 percent of the money. This indicates that a mere 10 percent of agents are so strongly motivated to achieve their goals that they can outdistance the other 90 percent. If you have the strength to push yourself 110 percent, you will be amazed at what you can achieve!

One way to develop this strength is by focusing 100 percent of your energy on something you really love, such as building a model airplane or playing a musical instrument. While focusing your mind intensely, you will be at peace, which facilitates clear positive thinking. Better connected to the source of your inspiration, you are apt to find *all* aspects of life less problematic and much more pleasant. This focus is true meditation.

Practicing quiet single-pointed meditation, or focused thought, is another way to attain a state of tranquillity that will overflow into motivation and enthusiasm. A common theme in many spiritual philosophies is the awareness of truth attained through being awake and focused exclusively on what is in front of us. The controlled, directed, focused thought that enables us to see truth can also eliminate fears, doubts, and other mental hindrances to achieving our goals. A well-controlled mind acts like a fierce warrior against negative emotions and limiting thoughts—the greatest enemies of success. In either case, whether you work with focused energy toward a goal or meditate to find your purpose in life, your mind will eventually achieve clarity and balance.

The Hazards of Procrastination

When you have something to do, tackle it right away. Don't think, "It will only take a minute—I'll do it later." Whenever possible, leave nothing for later. Why? Because procrastination leads to catastrophe. Subconsciously knowing that a job is waiting to be done will distract you from the task at hand, zapping your energy and compromising your productivity.

It is not long hard work that depletes our energy reserves, but rather daydreaming, fantasizing about pointless matters, or worrying about unfinished tasks instead of just getting them done. All the little things that remain undone can lead to our own undoing just as many small threads make up a thick rope that can one day be tied into a noose. Moreover, in divesting us of vital energy, procrastination also disempowers us. If the work will not be completed when expected, the job is apt to go to someone else who can do it more quickly.

Although energy quickly dissipates while we are thinking nonproductive thoughts, it never runs out when our thoughts are properly directed. In fact, the more attention we give to a task, the more empowered we will be to do it effectively and efficiently. The reason is that in training our scattered mind to focus on the "here and now," we develop a laserlike power to cut through our illusion of the world as a difficult place. Whereas procrastination keeps us vacillating like a seesaw, energy strongly focused moves us forward and thereby assures success.

High levels of success often come from combining focused energy with "doing for the sake of doing"—an important Buddhist teaching. This means first, doing whatever is in front of you, whether or not it is your job, and more significantly, doing the best job possible for the purpose of fulfilling a need rather than receiving credit. An opportunity to do for the sake of doing came my way one day when I was seventeen years old and working in a professional photo lab. One afternoon a client mentioned that he had two parties to photograph the same night and wondered if I would take the pictures for him at one of them. He said he would pay me $75 for the twelve-hour job. Seeing the jam he was in, I agreed to help out.

The party was held in a home, and as was my custom, I arrived early. The hostess, rushed for time, was vacuuming in a panic. Seeing that there was much to be done, I offered to help. I took the vacuum from her and set to work. Once the party started, I did my job as photographer, and afterward I helped clean up, much to the delight of the host and hostess. Then I left, never expecting to see them again.

About five years later, while working as a real estate agent, I presented a client's offer to purchase at the office of Mr. D., owner of the apartment building, who had a reputation for being ruthless in business. In response to the offer, Mr. D. arrived at a counterproposal, whereupon I returned to my client. He made a second offer, which required another visit to Mr. D. This time while I was sitting in his office, I noticed a portrait of a young boy and recognized it as a photograph I had taken. When I asked who the boy was, Mr. D. and I both flashed back to the party. He remembered how hard I worked that night and the extra effort I put in, remarking on my generosity. Again he rejected my client's offer, but he had another apartment building for sale which he offered to *me,* reducing the price from $170,000 to $140,000. Despite the attractive offer, the traditional 20 percent down payment was beyond my means. Wanting to help me advance in my career and considering me an "enthusiastic young man, sincere about doing a good job," Mr. D. asked what I could pay. I told him I had only $10,000 to my name, and he accepted. Furthermore, he carried the mortgage at a reduced interest rate and told me that if ever I had empty apartments and was unable to make a payment, he would drop the month's charges.

Six months later, the owners of the building next to the one I purchased from Mr. D. offered to buy my building for $235,000. So it was that taking a $75 job and doing what was in front of me, even though housecleaning was not in the photographer's line of duty, turned into a payoff that changed my life.

How to Reach Your Goal

The technique for acquiring anything we desire is first and foremost sincere and total devotion to the goal. When we are loyal to our goal, keys to achieving it will appear. This means that anyone, regardless of their socioeconomic background or educational level, can succeed.

To begin with, we must know what we want; then we must be willing to strive for it. Interestingly, we tend not to value material objects or even spiritual wisdom that is handed to us on a silver platter. The reason may well be that true value is ascribed only to goals we pour all our energy into accomplishing.

If you follow these instructions completely, and put your heart and faith in your goal, you will succeed:

1. **Focus on your goal.** Be as specific as possible. For instance, if your goal is a car, concentrate on the model and color; if it is money, focus on the exact amount. Your goal need not be limited to material objects—it could be peace of mind or climbing a mountain. To build confidence in this system and in yourself, start with a small goal and gradually work your way up to larger and more meaningful ones.

2. **See how you will reach the goal.** If your goal is an amount of money, determine how you will earn it. If it is a certain profession, map out how you will acquire the knowledge needed to gain entry into it. If it is climbing a mountain, develop a training program to hone your mountaineering skills. If you cannot see a way to get what you want, remain alert to opportunities and ideas that appear. The one that will fire you up might be something you never thought of before, or a long-forgotten plan you had as a child.

3. **Set a deadline for achieving your goal.** Be reasonable yet not too lenient. Remember, you are in control. Persist and feel confident that you will attain your desire before the deadline. In addition, see yourself as having already accomplished it and simply waiting to have it delivered by that date.

4. **Write an affirmative statement of your goal,** incorporating into it a definition, the means for attaining the goal, and your deadline. Here is an example:

   "By June 1 of next year I will trek thirty days through the Himalayas in Nepal. I will exercise a minimum of one hour every day to build physical strength, and start saving as much as possible so I will have $10,000 to pay for the trip. There is no doubt or question in my mind that I will achieve this goal by June 1. It is mine—I can see myself in the mountains, I can feel the money for the trip in my hands. I am totally devoted to achieving my goal, and I will not slack off in my efforts to achieve it. I am open to changing my line of work and other aspects of my life in order to succeed in fulfilling this dream."

5. **Repeat your affirmative statement out loud** a few times every morning and night until you have it memorized. Continue to repeat it with as much feeling as possible day after day until you can clearly see the object of desire in your possession. Verbal repetition is a proven method for imprinting information in the mind. It has an effect similar to repeatedly listening to the same song on the radio or reading a book out loud, which prompts far better recall than reading it silently. Pilots in training, for instance, are taught to name aloud every item on a checklist of equipment while touching each one to ensure alertness and thoroughness.

This system helped me sell a $22,000,000 building before my self-imposed deadline while I was a young and inexperienced real estate agent. Not only was this a very large sale for a newcomer to the industry, but it involved a building in downtown Montreal, where for two years nearly every broker had known it was on the market. For some reason it seemed to be waiting for me. The opportunity appeared unexpectedly one day when a broker asked me to check out a building with a store for rent that might be suitable for one of his clients. The broker himself did not have time to spend on a deal yielding such a small commission, but for me no deal was too small. So I went to see the store, and quite to my surprise met the owner there. After realizing that we could not make a deal on the rental, I asked him if he wanted to buy something big. The rest, as they say, is history.

What possessed the broker to send me there? What caused me to accept such a potentially unrewarding assignment? What compelled me to mention the multimillion-dollar building while checking on a rental? Why had this wealthy investor not known the building was for sale? The answer to all these questions is this: when we build the fire and fan the flames of our plan, we become inspired to act in ways that will bring it to fruition. The universe also does what it can to help out.

Transforming Sexual Energy

The human sex drive is such a strong instinct that it can distract the mind from paying attention to other important aspects of life. Yet sexual desire can also be transformed into an energy that fuels the strength, creativity, and persistence needed to attain a goal. Many Eastern mystical traditions explicitly guide practitioners through this transformation for purposes of achieving increased physical and spiritual capacities; indeed, entire volumes have been written on this subject. But it is also true that these same procedures can yield an abundant harvest in the practical day-to-day quest to achieve our goals.

To harness the power of your sexuality, observe and recognize your feelings of sexual desire, differentiating them from other energies. Then identify the object of your desire—the person you'd like to have sexual intercourse with. When sexual desire is strong, mentally replace this person with your chosen goal and use the same force of emotion to bring about your new objective, all the while transmuting the object of your desire without necessarily having sex. Redirecting this powerful energy to your goal can provide the self-discipline and energy levels needed to succeed.

Once you have sufficiently strengthened your will forces, you will be able to build sexual desire whenever you choose *without* involving another person or becoming sexually aroused. By focusing your mind on your goal and then concentrating on the feeling of sexual energy, you will be able to invite the creative power of your entire being to enter into your quest. From there it is likely to propel you to great heights of success. Patience is required, however, since this ability develops over time and with considerable practice in sensing subtle feelings as sexual essence begins to build.

What determines whether its power destroys or creates is the refinement and focus you bring to it through self-discipline. According to the Talmud, "Man has an organ; the more he feeds it, the hungrier it gets." This is the danger of sex. If you are unconscious of your desires, they may overpower you and take you on distracting side roads that lead nowhere—all the while consuming prodigious amounts of energy—or even worse, they may end up hurting another person. So exercise caution while using this energy. You need not be celibate; just be wise.

Overcoming Obstacles

Even when we are devoted to success, whether in business, spiritual growth, or skydiving, other desires can distract us from achieving our goal. We may become so preoccupied with these diversions that we are unable to maintain the focus or energy required to move forward. The culprits at such times are the many I's that like to demoralize us and keep us busy through "active laziness." Yet if we would concentrate on achieving our primary goal, the distractions would dissipate. Mahatma Gandhi said it this way: "Man often becomes what he believes himself to be. If I keep on saying to myself that I cannot do a certain thing, it is possible that I may end by really becoming incapable of doing it. On the contrary, if I have the belief that I can do it, I shall surely acquire the capacity to do it even if I may not have it at the beginning."

For practical mystics, active laziness—the pursuit of many unnecessary time- and energy-absorbing activities—becomes a means of approaching their goal, for it forces them to evaluate why they are not achieving their objective. They regard the obstacles it poses as tests that can be used to ascertain how determined they really are to deeply understand their desire, like a parent who waits to see if their child's longing to play an expensive instrument is serious before making the purchase. The advantages of obstacles is illustrated by the following story of a Zen sword master.

Once upon a time, a young Japanese man named Hiroshi wished to learn the way of the sword. He approached a Zen sword master and asked to be accepted as a disciple. The master agreed, with the traditional condition that Hiroshi do exactly as he was told without question. Hiroshi accepted.

As is often the case, the new disciple was given menial tasks to perform. After a year of cooking and dishwashing, with not a single sword lesson, Hiroshi approached the master and asked when his training would begin. The master replied, "You are not yet ready. The training will begin in time." After another year passed, Hiroshi became frustrated. Again he approached the master, only to receive the same reply. Nonetheless, Hiroshi decided to stay on and follow through with his responsibilities.

Shortly afterward, the master started coming up from behind Hiroshi and hitting him with a broomstick as he was washing dishes. Sometimes, out of the blue he would throw a pot at Hiroshi, knocking him flat on his face. Respect for the master kept Hiroshi from complaining. After a month of this treatment, he started to hear sounds just when he was about to be struck, but he was too late in responding. Eventually, he could hear the master enter the room and was able to turn and face him before the surprise attack.

Finally, the day of Hiroshi's first official sword lesson arrived. He was apprehensive about what might happen since being a cook had proven so dangerous. To his surprise, despite never having handled a sword in battle,

Hiroshi was instinctively able to block every strike, responding instantly as the master began each move. And thus, Hiroshi became a great swordsman by patiently washing dishes.

Just as Hiroshi knew in advance that his time as a cook was limited, so can we learn to see obstruction as limited. Viewing an obstacle as an unending barrier will deter us from pursuing our goal; viewing it as a translucent sheet of paper, however, will keep us moving forward. When we are able to perceptually turn a continuing impediment into a minor hurdle, we will have no qualms about jumping over it, or going around or through it. Odd as it may sound, adversity can sometimes be our greatest asset. The strength we develop in overcoming it is often just what is needed to realize our dreams.

Preventing Failure

We can spend twenty years overcoming obstacles and building up a fortune, and in one day lose it all. For this reason, we must learn what to look out for so as to prevent a catastrophe—tips we can glean from others. But unfortunately, few of us avail ourselves of such information. A friend may tell us about the problems he had in realizing his dreams, whereupon we will proceed to make the same mistakes and suffer the same consequences.

We are led to repeat others' failures by our arrogance—a sense that we are better than them, or that they are mere fools. And so it is *we* who become the fools, reinventing the wheel only to be run over by it.

To gain insight from others' experiences, we might begin by talking to bitter elderly people who have made mistakes. They are excellent teachers of pitfalls to avoid. If we also talk to happy elderly people, we will find they, too, have made mistakes but have reacted differently. Learning about the successes and failures of our elders, then, offers us the twin rewards of time-tested wisdom and personal insights—including glimpses into the differences between people who persisted and those who gave up. It is regrettable that we

Westerners have so little respect for our elders that we confine them to retirement homes. In so doing, we deprive ourselves of an invaluable resource for easing our lives and increasing our chances of success.

As you explore the worldly side of life, learn how to circumvent difficulties so that you will not risk losing all that you will have worked to build. For starters, steer clear of these land mines:

❖ Being afraid of what you think you cannot change;

❖ Listening to and believing people's negative messages about you;

❖ Giving up before you finish;

❖ Deciding that you are not good enough, or that someone else can attain your goal better than you can;

❖ Worrying about what others will think of you if you fail.

In the event that you do meet with failure, face it with equanimity. An interviewer once asked Thomas Edison, inventor of the electric lightbulb, how he went on after failing ten thousand times. Edison replied, "I never failed once. I discovered ten thousand things that did not work." Indeed, you, too, will never fail as long as you know that you are gaining from every action you take. And in retrospect, knowing *what* you have gained is as important as knowing *that* you have gained.

This principle of viewing failure as a stepping stone to success applies to every aspect of life, and helps us achieve a variety of goals. For example, past relationships are often viewed as failures, which is never the case; they were simply learning experiences to prepare us for more successful relationships. As British author George Bernard Shaw once said, "When I was young, I observed that nine out of every ten things I did were failures, so I did ten times more work."

History is replete with examples of people persisting against great odds. For example, in the 1940s Mahatma Gandhi refused to let adversity squelch his dream. Although jailed, beaten, and ridiculed, he re-mained humble and unembittered, never giving up his fight for the freedom of his people, which in the end he won.

Hence achieving success necessitates not only reprogramming our minds to eliminate the thought of failing but also seeing life as a constant progression toward success. When we view life from this perspective, we gain vast amounts of energy for waking up.

Ways to Increase Your Energy Level

The energy that runs our bodies, our machines, the world, and the universe is similar in one respect: the more of it there is, the better and longer things will work. In terms of our bodies, energy levels determine our mood and our ability to allocate time to personally meaningful pursuits. Ultimately, the amount of energy that is available to us relates directly to how we will experience our life and how much we will profit from it.

The business world offers this useful equation: The best way to increase profit is to lower expenses rather than increase sales. It would be of no benefit to increase sales if expenses increased at an equal or greater rate, since we would only end up working harder for the same amount of money, being disillusioned, and feeling that life is pointless. In terms of personal vitality, this means that reducing the amount of energy expended needlessly will leave more available for pursuing your true desires.

One way to minimize energy expenditure is by maintaining consistency in attitudes and actions. For example, if you act differently toward coworkers, friends, and family, you are using three different operating systems, switching constantly from one to another throughout the course of each day. Imagine how much energy it would take to use three different operating systems on your computer, switching back and forth between them every few hours. By contrast, if you bring the *same* attitudes and behaviors to all your spheres of endeavor, you will have more energy available for other endeavors. Expending less energy in day-to-day living, you will need less time to sleep and recover energy, which will leave you more time to accomplish your goals.

Following are more ideas for reducing the amount of energy needlessly expended and for increasing your energy reserves:

◆ **Know when to eat.** Do you realize how affected you are by hunger? With a decrease in nutrients stored in the body, energy levels drop and productivity falls off. Therefore, at the first sign of hunger reach for food—preferably healthy, natural sources of nutrition. To prepare in advance for your food needs, store a sandwich or snack in the car if you expect to be out all day, or keep raw vegetables in your briefcase. For maximum energy, eat enough to satisfy your hunger but do not stuff yourself. Strive for light foods and small meals, since large heavy meals will promote drowsiness and listlessness.

◆ **Lighten your load.** Minimize the number of items you carry. Use the smallest possible briefcase, backpack, purse, or agenda book. Do not haul a lot of stuff around in the event that you *might* need it. In deciding whether an item goes with you or stays, adhere to this guideline: If you didn't use it last week, you probably won't need it. The less you carry, the less you will have to think about, which will free up more mental energy for creativity.

In addition, dispose of old notes and other papers you are finished with. Clean out and organize your desk, drawers, and other spots where useless items accumulate; then discard everything that does not pertain to your current life goals. To guard against future accumulations of worthless items, repeat this cleanup weekly. Piles of unwanted paraphernalia can weigh you down with discouragement every time you look at them.

◆ **Do less.** Reduce the amount of unnecessary work you do in a day. At times, the "work" most productive might be a walk in the woods, a weekend of camping in the mountains, or any other form of recreation that relaxes the mind and recharges the body.

Eliminate all nonproductive or destructive activities, whether they are related to business or pleasure. Also cut out potentially useless trips. Confirm appointments in advance to avoid wasting time waiting, and between appointments take advantage of spare moments to rest, read, or meditate. The meditation practice of following your breath, described on page 160, is possible anywhere, at any time. When you feel filled with energy, use it to attain a state of balance in the moment.

◆ **Associate with inspiring people.** Spend your time with people who elevate you, and stay away from those who deflate you. If a person cannot "get their act together," reconsider socializing with them. Veer away from negative-minded people and those who thrive on gossip or slander. Instead, seek out individuals with the highest moral standards. But be careful not to isolate yourself. From time to time, sit and read at a cafe, do volunteer work, or visit stimulating places—in other words, remain accessible to the opportunities life may present. The universe will not overnight these to your door; rather, it will deliver them when the time is ripe.

If while applying this principle you lose some friends, understand that in time you will have new, more compatible friends. To optimize your mental reprogramming, prepare to let go of all draining relationships so that invigorating ones can take their place. Remember, if you want to be with a "ten," you must *be* a ten.

◆ **Delegate tasks.** Managers delegate; production people do the hands-on work. If you're on the way up the managerial ladder, now is the time to learn to delegate. Don't think you're the only one who can get the job done, even if you *can* do it better than others; while another person does that job, you can be working on something more important. The function of the boss is to do nothing but delegate, saving energy for the most critical tasks. Delegating successfully, however, calls for trust and an ability to release the controlling lesser ego. In fact, 90 percent of the impending bankruptcies I have consulted on involved an owner trying to control all operations, even after the firm had grown beyond one person's ability to guide.

To circumvent this problem, remember that the world needs all types of people to complete a variety of jobs. While dealing with coworkers or employees whose performance does not measure up to your expectations, try not to get discouraged or frustrated. Rather, learn to communicate patiently with them in their own language, and finish what needs to be done.

◆ **Be on time.** Arrive on time or early for all appointments. Busy, successful people do not like to work with latecomers. Being on time—in personal as well as business situations—shows respect for others, implies that you value their time, and conserves energy otherwise wasted in rushing and feeling nervous about being late.

◆ **Speak less.** Say what needs to be said, precisely and concisely. Minimize not only your talks with others but also your own internal dialogues. To begin, try cutting out unnecessary repetition and focusing only on what is important—in other words, go on a speech diet. Recommended by virtually all mystical teachings, this practice will not only help you conserve energy but also quiet your mind enough to concentrate on what is going on around you. In addition, a speech diet will strengthen your willpower and free up surprising amounts of time.

◆ **Exercise.** Physical exercise gets the heart pumping, which increases blood flow throughout the body, boosting energy levels and sharpening brain functions. With daily practice, you are sure to notice results rather quickly.

To sustain high energy levels, I do Qi Gong and Tai Chi—Chinese disciplines that teach mental focus and physical flexibility. After twelve weeks of practicing these movements for an hour a day, one of my students decreased her sleep needs from ten to six hours a night, all the while increasing her energy reserves. Chapter 10 provides descriptions of some of these exercises, although the best way to learn them is from a qualified master who has honed the attributes you seek to acquire.

Nine Steps to Success

As you can see, success in this world hinges on much more—and in some ways, much less—than painstaking nose-to-the-grindstone work. It requires everything from an honest appraisal of motivation to an understanding of negativity and energy flow. In practical terms, manifesting a dream calls for nine simple actions:

1. **Focus on your goal.** Clearly define your objective. Write a detailed statement about it, including the date you will achieve it and the actions you will take. Memorize this statement and repeat it as often as possible, especially upon waking and before going to sleep. (See page 53.)

2. **Be aware** of what is happening 360 degrees around you, as well as above and below. Opportunities can appear anywhere. A heightened awareness will also tune you into your intuition.

3. **Have faith** that you will succeed no matter how long it takes. Listen to your heart and soul rather than your doubting mind. Believe without question that your goal is already within reach. Let doubts and negative thoughts bounce off your mental umbrella.

4. **Be considerate and compassionate** toward all forms of life that you affect directly or indirectly. People, animals, and plants

deserve respect. So, too, do inanimate objects, since they represent the efforts of their makers and owners. Remember that everything in existence was created by someone. In giving respect, you cultivate self-respect.

5. **Sustain a burning desire** to reach your goal. Be willing to do anything that won't hurt others. Use your mind constructively and allow emotion to saturate your thoughts and visions of success. To sustain the flow of emotion, the magic ingredient that turns efforts into successes, visualize your true motivation. If, for example, your desire is to earn money to support your family, see your family and feel your love for them whenever you experience discouragement or obstruction.

6. **Maintain daily discipline** on your chosen path. Make at least one effort toward achieving your goal every day, no matter what the day brings; writing down your efforts in the evening will remind you that you are being persistent and deserve success, or that you need to try harder. Persistence expresses your faith and devotion.

7. **Accept responsibility** for all your actions and those of your employees. Never make excuses.

8. **Associate only with people you admire.** Interact with people who inspire you, and pay no attention to negative statements from others or to what they may think of you. Emulate those you wish to be like.

9. **Do the best you can** for the sake of a positive outcome rather than for acknowledgment. Do not be concerned about receiving credit or recognition for what you do. Just do your best, then feel content with the role you have played in a job well done.

Chapter 5

How to Make Money

I bargained with Life for a penny,
And Life would pay no more,
However I begged at evening,
When I counted my scanty store.

For Life is a just employer,
It gives you what you ask,
But once you have set the wages,
Why, you must bear the task.

I worked for a laborer's wages,
Only to learn, dismayed,
That any wage I had asked of Life,
Life would have willingly paid.

This poem is not just about making money or achieving success in a chosen mission; it is about refining and focusing the scattered human mind. The life of practical mystics is much the same. By cultivating a wise relationship to money, a commodity so prevalent in today's world, and by determining exactly what they want, they gain both improved finances and a more disciplined mind.

Whether rich or poor, people worry about money. A wealthy man is concerned about his estate and his possessions. He worries about potential disasters, such as his house burning down, robbers breaking in, or kidnappers abducting him. He frets over death and the disposition of his wealth. A poor man suffers from insufficiency, which fuels endless desires for land, shelter, food, and clothing. He wears out both body and mind worrying about money.

Our goal as aspiring practical mystics is to attain financial freedom—liberation from the suffering imposed by wealth or poverty. As we move in this direction, there are two major points to consider. First, while increasing our income substantially, say to $100,000 a year, it is helpful to live as if we were still earning $10,000. By neglecting to do so, and increasing our expenses as we increase our income, we may never climb out of debt. Although we will have better toys, we will need to work just as hard as before. This is not the way to freedom.

Second, to be financially free, we must build up sufficient capital so that when opportunities arise we will have money to invest. Although it takes self-control to accumulate such funds, wise investments can provide a substantial income, freeing us from a five-day workweek. When our investments earn us enough money to live on 50 percent of the net income they generate, rather than spend the extra 50 percent, we can allocate it wisely. It can go toward increasing our financial base for bigger and more diversified investments, for instance, or toward fulfilling our benevolent desires, all the while being substantially useful to society as well.

If you set as your goal the mere accumulation of money rather than financial freedom, beware of developing an addiction to money. Once you have achieved your goal, know when to stop; otherwise, you may run the risk of becoming a workaholic incapable of enjoying the fruits of your labor. Money is the most dangerous of all addictions, because society's message that more is better serves to reinforce the habit. So be vigilant—don't let your desire for money drive you to extremes. Your sweat and toil will have been all for naught if your family life suffers from your absence or stress from overwork leads to ill health.

Financial Exercises

The following exercises, although perhaps difficult, can move you well along the path to financial freedom. Persist and you will not only excel in money management but also cultivate self-control and equanimity.

Exercise 5–1

Where Is My Money Going?

Every day for the next three months, list every cent you spend, even for a pack of gum. At the end of each month, add up your earnings and your expenses. The difference should be exactly what you have in savings (in addition to the amount you started with). This exercise fosters good bookkeeping skills and, more importantly, a consciousness of where your money is going, which is vital to awakening.

To take your financial finesse to the next level, after one or two months of recording your expenses, note where you are spending too much money and try to reduce these expenditures. For example, if you find you are spending $100 a week on an unnecessary item, try allocating only $80 a week to it over the next month. Once you are accustomed to spending $80 a week for it, try spending only $60. Continue this practice until you reach the absolute minimum you can spend on that item. In reviewing your expenses, also decide if any items or services can be eliminated. By gradually changing your lifestyle, you will find it easier to cut expenses to a bare minimum and thereby increase your wealth.

Exercise 5–2

Cutting Back on Expenses

Evaluate your lifestyle for any routine that is draining your finances and decreasing your productivity—such as smoking cigarettes, drinking alcohol, using recreational drugs, gambling, or sitting around drinking coffee. Create a plan to eliminate the routine, and document the resulting savings.

Items such as cigarettes, alcohol, and drugs result in a triple loss, since they drain our bank accounts, consume precious time and energy, and take a serious toll on our health. One man I know calculated his cigarette expenses for the year and found that they were equivalent to a week of occupancy in a five-star hotel in Hawaii plus first-class airfare to get there.

Exercise 5–3

Going on a Financial Diet

Regardless of your income, before making a purchase, ask yourself, "Do I need this for my survival?" Refuse to spend money on anything that does not contribute to your basic survival, thus eliminating such extravagances as vacations, new clothes, dinners in expensive restaurants, and spontaneous puchases. Explain to your friends that you are trying to get out of debt, and that while you are on this financial diet you cannot afford to be as generous as you used to be. If you are in debt, you may need to do this exercise for a year or two, depending on how much you earn and how much debt you need to clear.

While you are on your financial diet, replace activities that cost money with those you can do for free. Free forms of entertainment, for example, could be hiking or biking. Instead of paying expensive health club memberships, why not create an at-home exercise program that requires no special equipment? A hundred years ago there were no health clubs; a thousand years ago there was no exercise equipment; all this time, Eastern martial artists were in excellent physical condition. Hundreds of forms of free exercise can keep you fit aerobically as well, including yoga, Tai Chi, lifting rocks, shoveling snow, cutting the lawn with a manual mower, and a self-styled exercise program.

Exercise 5–4

Clarifying Your Goal

Visualize your goal, then draw a picture of it or cut one out of a magazine. Every day, mentally fill the picture with your thoughts of success until the goal has sprung to life. For example, if you want a new car, each time you gaze at the picture see the image of your car, and see yourself in the driver's seat. Repeat this exercise several times a day to form and retain a clear vision of your goal, making sure you are in it.

Exercise 5–5

Supplementing Your Income

Do whatever comes your way to earn money. If you have no special plans for a Saturday night and the opportunity arises to do an odd job, take it rather than going to the movies or surfing the Internet. During the week, find a part-time evening job instead of reading a novel or watching TV. Use your weekends, too, to earn a few extra dollars. However, don't get involved in get-rich-quick schemes. The only people who seem to get rich from these are the ones who came up with them in the first place.

You may need to practice this exercise for a few months, or even years, until your cash reserves are big enough to help you attain your goal. I started at age thirteen and for eleven years worked straight through, including Christmas and New Year's Day. But over that period of time I also went from nothing to a net worth of close to a million dollars.

While practicing exercise 5–5, once you have accumulated a sufficient amount of money to invest, explore your options. Rather than put your savings into someone else's business, for example, consider starting one of your own that can eventually provide an income without much direct effort on your part. Of course, you will have to work hard to build the business, which may take several years.

Choose Positive Thoughts

Even though on one level we may want money, negative thoughts can prevent us from acquiring it. Many people do not have money despite their desire for it because their underlying belief is that money is bad and rich folks are obnoxious, or are "hoarding" the world's wealth. Other people harbor a subconscious fear of money, convinced that they will be unable to withstand such corruption. Money in itself, however, is not bad; the objections arise from what people *do* with money.

Money is simply a tool to help us achieve our goals. Therefore, accept and use it beneficially while remaining aware of how it can affect the lesser ego and while keeping your heart pure and your focus on your goal.

Religious teachings differ in their advice on wealth. The New Testament tells us: "It is easier to pass a rope [sometimes translated as 'camel'] through the eye of a needle than for a rich man to get into heaven." Similarly, the path of the fakir—a mendicant acknowledged by many traditions—views poverty and self-mortification as a vehicle for spiritual growth. Judaism, on the other hand, considers wealth a necessity for doing what we believe in, since it frees us from having to depend on others to meet our basic needs. Furthermore, a Hindu teaching states that we must have wealth, property, sex, and other worldly pleasures in this life so that we can see the futility of them all, and thereby free ourselves of desire. (*Note:* One can easily get lost on this Hindu path, which is probably why it is not commonly taught.)

Despite their differing viewpoints, religious teachings agree that what counts in spiritual growth is *attitude*. If upon acquiring wealth you can continually remind yourself that you are the same person as before, you are the same as everyone else, and your wealth is for the purpose of attaining a humanitarian goal rather than power over others, then you will use it wisely. Heaven will indeed open its doors to one who has worked so hard to help so many.

Whether or not you are guided by religious teachings, beware of confusing your image of money with the arrogance, jealousy, and envy of some rich people. Such attitudes have sprung from society's treatment of them, which nurtured their lesser ego. You do not have to fall into this soul-degrading trap, but you do have to watch your step.

Above all, remember that our thoughts affect 95 percent of the outcome of our lives. This means that if we cannot control our thoughts, we have only a 5 percent chance of success. Your primary objective must therefore be to keep your thoughts about money as positive as possible. To move in this direction, do not get lost in distractions, watch your senses and the impressions you expose yourself to, and fill your mind with thoughts of positive value.

Eastern and Western religions alike tell us, "All creatures are created equal, with one exception—man. God gave man freedom of choice." Each of us is a thinking, living being with the capacity to choose. Not to use this gift is to deny ourselves the chance of having a fulfilling, happy, peaceful life as well as an opportunity to be useful to society.

While choosing your path in life, observe the following guidelines and regularly practice exercise 5–6 below:

❖ Do only what you believe in with all your heart. Even if in a roundabout way an action might benefit someone or something you love, consider it worthy of your efforts.

❖ Question everything with an open mind—the mind of a child who has no preconceived notions or judgments. Do not refute or dispute ideas for the sake of arguing.

❖ Never adopt a concept on faith alone. Assume it may be true, then prove its validity for yourself.

❖ Accept that you know nothing. You will then realize there is something to learn from everyone, and you will begin to listen with a receptive mind. Once you have absorbed new information, decide if you wish to apply it to your life. The universe is in a constant state of transformation. Hence assuming that what you already know will be relevant for the rest of your life is ill-advised since it would keep you from evolving as a result of increased knowledge.

Exercise 5–6

Clearing Out Negativity

To remove negative thoughts about money from the deepest levels of your subconscious, repeat while visualizing your objective: "Money is neither good nor bad; it is simply a means of achieving my goal."

Boosting Your Chances of Success in Business

Starting a business is an exciting adventure. To increase your chances of success, focus on refining your personality to earn respect from yourself as well as others. Also familiarize yourself with the product or service you are offering, and understand the psychology of the people you are dealing with.

Respect is based largely on the reliability of your word, or as my grandfather used to remark, "A man's worth is calculated by his word." If you say you will be at a certain place at a particular time, make sure you are there. Should it be impossible to honor the commitment, call well in advance to explain your delay. If you tell someone to expect a call from you tomorrow, then make the call— even if only to say you're too busy to talk and need to reschedule the conversation. In addition to staying true to your word, communicate clearly and accurately. Sincerely mean every word you say. To develop these skills, practice the following exercise.

Exercise 5–7

Say What You Mean and Mean What You Say

Pay attention to your words, noticing whether or not they are truthful. If you catch yourself lying, recognize that you are hurting yourself the most. Consider that you may be speaking on "automatic pilot"; then try to become more conscious of thinking before you talk. Taking charge of the words you use is the best way there is to honor them and thereby cultivate self-respect.

To increase your chances of honoring your commitments, only make a promise if you know you can keep it without pressuring yourself. If you are not prepared to do so, exercise restraint before speaking. To assist in your efforts, keep a notepad by the phone or in your pocket for jotting down "to do" notes, and remember to check them. The reason for avoiding pressure is that tension consumes enormous amounts of energy. Although while under pressure you may initially experience an adrenaline rush, you will eventually feel drained. The bigger the pressure, the greater the release . . . and the longer the recovery period.

Honoring our word serves many purposes. For one, it enhances our credibility, inspiring people to give us opportunities to attain our goals. For another, it strengthens our self-discipline and willpower—invaluable tools in all aspects of life. Honoring our word also builds self-respect. Every time we fail to keep a commitment, we feel bad and either consciously or subconsciously lose a little more respect for ourselves, ultimately sabotaging our chances for success. Losing self-respect is somewhat like living in a city and after a while not hearing the traffic. Although you don't notice it, the background noise still affects you, even while you sleep.

In addition to honoring your word, become intimately knowledgeable about the product or service you are providing. The more knowledge you acquire, the more confidence it will instill in your clients. Show them that you are in control of your business activities by answering their questions honestly and accurately. When necessary, admit that you are not sure of the correct answer but will find it quickly. Hand in hand with knowing your trade, know yourself. Honesty and dependability, together with knowledge and skills, form the cornerstones of good business.

Understanding the psychology of employees and potential clients is more difficult than acquiring knowledge about a product or service, yet it can significantly increase the success of your business. Since words often have many different meanings, we need to carefully choose the terms we use and speak in a way that will convey our true thoughts. While talking to people who are fidgeting or looking confused, we should stop and ask if they understand our message. At such times, rephrasing our statements may be to everyone's advantage.

Business meetings, whether they are in an office, at a restaurant, or at a dinner party, require psychological finesse. In fact, what we are selling is often not only a product or service but also our personality. In small deals involving the sale of inexpensive items or labor, clients are looking for a competitive price. In large deals related to real estate, stocks, or corporate transactions, where there is stiffer competition and more complex and long-term arrangements, clients are paying more attention to such factors as relationship and comfort level.

Following are thirteen basic guidelines to adopt when dealing with human psychology in your business startup:

◆ **Show your respect.** Treat clients like close friends and view all deals as equally important. The amount of money involved is irrelevant—$100 will be as important to one client as $1,000,000 will be to another. So, do not dismiss small deals; they may lead to bigger ones in the future. Remember the $75 photography job that yielded a $95,000 payoff and the $1,000 lease that led to a $22,000,000 sale, both of which were described in chapter 4.

◆ **Complete projects.** Bring all deals to a mutually beneficial conclusion. When a project leaves you with a commission that is only a fraction of what the client made or what you expected, do not feel cheated or jealous. Instead, know that since you have done a good job the client may want you involved in the next deal. What results in a good reputation and repeat business is prompt and efficient service.

Efficiency in completing a job or service can often be enhanced by delegating work. Even though our egos may have us striving to control everything, we must be willing to let others use *their* expertise when it is superior to our own. Working humbly with people who know more than we do has the added benefit of increasing our knowledge. Of course, if you are in a managerial position, delegating is always the path to efficiency, as we saw earlier.

When we fulfill our duties to the best of our ability, we reap the satisfaction of having contributed to a fine outcome. Martin Luther King once said: "If your job is to clean the streets, then do it with all your heart because that is your job. Do it so well that when people walk down that street they comment that the person who cleaned that street really did a wonderful job." No matter how insignificant the final result may seem, when we do our best we enhance our self-esteem. And our efforts will certainly be acknowledged, although the recognition may take time and come from an unexpected source. Even if all we gain is enhanced self-esteem, that should be good enough.

◆ **Reserve your personal beliefs.** What you believe, feel, value, trust, and understand is of no relevance. Yet what you believe, feel, value, trust, and understand is of the utmost importance. Although these statements may sound contradictory, they are not.

Personal beliefs are irrelevant to business affairs because they tend to come from the lesser ego, which must be kept under control. When we believe we know something, we want to show off our knowledge—which is the lesser ego's way of saying, "Look at me"—yet even though we may be right, others will view us as braggarts. Although we might not think much of an item or see potential in a project, if a client does, that is what counts. Rather than make business decisions on the basis of personal opinion, it is better to remain open-minded and receptive to the *client's* beliefs.

Personal morals and values are best kept private while interacting with business colleagues as well. If they indulge in behaviors we find offensive, it is not our place to lecture. In the business world, we should see ourselves as humble servants who do not pass judgment on others, although we certainly retain the right to control our own environment.

One morning when I was managing a large real estate portfolio, for example, I had to pick up my boss at his home. As he approached the car, I noticed he was smoking a cigar, and since I did not allow people to smoke in my home or car I politely asked him to put out the noxious fumes. This highly influential man, obviously unaccustomed to being told what to do, paused a moment in shock and then extinguished the cigar. After several minutes of silence, he said, "I admire a strong man." A year later this man, who had been paying me a pittance to manage his properties, offered me a contract for $500,000 a year to manage a new twenty-story apartment building development. The car incident and subsequent requests made in defense of my environment had convinced him that this kid was not one to be easily intimidated when the pressure was on.

Although on one level personal beliefs other than those relating directly to your environment are irrelevant to business affairs, on another level they are enormously relevant. Because you have gained knowledge through years of experience in business, and because clients are dealing with you *on account of* your expertise, when you see potential profit or danger for them, you owe it to them to voice your feelings. Do this humbly, however, to avoid unleashing the lesser ego's desire to put down others in order to elevate itself. If the lesser ego does come to the fore, the quality of your advice is likely to diminish, perhaps leading to disastrous consequences. If your lesser ego remains uninvolved and your humble opinion ends up angering a client, refrain from commenting or getting upset. Instead, take the opportunity to practice self-observation and develop willpower by refusing to resort to negative, retaliatory actions.

In stating your understanding, do not modify your morals or values to suit your clients. In fact, to discourage them from making snap judgments about you, reveal little, if anything, about yourself. Let them get to know you before forming a clear opinion of you. The best way to relate to people in business is to answer questions directly and in as few words as possible—an ability fostered by the speech diet referred to on page 62. Also ask as many questions as you wish about your clients' opinions on the subject or on related issues; this way you will learn, others will be happy talking about what they love, and doors will open. Limited speaking—found among the great practices taught by Sufis, Pythagoras, as well as in the Kaballah, the Hermetica, and Buddhist scripture—aids us in our inner growth as well as in our material life.

Whether you are humbly sharing your personal beliefs or keeping them to yourself, be sincere. This practice is likely to attract associates and clients who want money in order to provide a better life for themselves and others, as opposed to people who are acting purely out of self-interest and greed. For best results all around, always be sincere, regardless of other people's motivations.

◆ **Be conversant in a variety of topics.** Clients want to see that you are intelligent and knowledgeable about a broad range of subjects.

In one sense, having a common interest outside of your business dealings can promote a friendly relationship to cement your professional ties. In another, discussions of this sort can help cultivate you as a person, enabling you to develop all sides of your being.

When there is an opening in a conversation, speak modestly and unpretentiously if you are familiar with the subject, but stay silent if you know nothing about it. If you try to talk about a topic you know nothing about, you will sound like a fool. A wise and humble individual admits to being unfamiliar with a subject, asks questions, and lets others speak.

◆ **Accept criticism graciously.** When there is a chance you may be wrong, receive criticism with equanimity and welcome offerings of new information. If these traits are not already part of your character, strive to cultivate them. In the process you will be conquering the lesser ego, developing humility, increasing your knowledge and skills, and making a better first impression. Refining these simple traits is enough to cause a major growth spurt in the evolving soul of the aspiring practical mystic.

◆ **Know when to speak and when to be silent**. When you have something to say, look into the eyes of the person as you speak to them. If you are addressing several people, look directly into the eyes of one person for a few seconds, then move on to the next, and so forth. Eye-to-eye and heart-to-heart contact will inform you of your listeners' reactions and will ensure that everyone is included in the conversation.

If someone you are speaking with puts a negative slant on the conversation, it is not necessarily up to you to turn it around. In attempting to do so, you may only end up stopping them from venting their animosity. Hence it is better to simply not participate, letting the negativity dissolve upon its release. Think of water passing from a reservoir through a hose. If the end of the hose were suddenly plugged up, pressure would build; but if it were to remain unplugged, the water would run out of the hose and the reservoir would eventually dry up. So it is for a person spouting negativity.

For your part, the best course of action is to be like a mountain, unmoved by and unresponsive to the negative words. Through silence, we permit others to release their animosity. Ultimately, we do this not so much for them as for ourselves, since refusing to be buffeted by the winds of negativity keeps us on our path of balance.

◆ **Accept responsibility for your actions.** If you have made a mistake and are being paid by the hour, do not charge for the time it takes to fix the problem you created. People who suffer a financial loss because of someone else's error are infuriated by such extra fees. To keep business dealings clean and to act with integrity, it is much more advantageous to correct your mistakes at your own expense. Even if you lose money in the process, you will gain more in terms of respect and future business.

◆ **Be considerate.** People and machines have one thing in common: they will not perform well if you push the wrong buttons. To deepen your understanding of others' psychological "buttons," explore your own by paying attention to what is going on in and around you. Observe your reactions—learn who you really are by sensing the feelings in your body. Only when you truly know yourself can you be considerate of others. Until then, remember this: Good judgment comes from experience; experience comes from bad judgment.

◆ **Stay calm.** Keep your financial transactions as even-tempered as possible. If you expect the price of an item to be ten dollars and it turns out to be one thousand dollars, don't let your expression register shock or declare that the price is beyond your limit. Instead, calmly say, "No thank you," or "I'll consider it." In non-financial dealings, too, it is best to avoid showing undue excitement. Act as if whatever you are told is what you expected. In short, do not let your lesser ego cause you to react emotionally and childishly. Instead, strive for equanimity.

◆ **Maintain a positive outlook.** No matter what a situation entails, see it in a beneficial light, remembering that seemingly massive obstacles often turn out to be the best catapults to a goal. If a problem arises and others fear the outcome, point out positive aspects of the situation that are both realistic and practical. As a result, these people will want to be with you more often and take your advice to heart. Seeing everything as an asset rather than a liability is an effective business tool and an invaluable character trait.

An exchange I once had with a man from England illustrates how a positive outlook can affect success. The man was in the security business, and we discussed the possibility of his setting up a similar venture in the United States. He perceived a major impasse since he did not know how things worked in the States, but I saw his situation differently: although he did not know the American way, Americans did not know his way and would welcome new ideas and talents. As it turned out, his greatest perceived obstacle was in fact his most pronounced asset. His knowledge joined with his open-mindedness to launch a huge success.

While explaining why a perceived obstacle could be of benefit, express enthusiasm without overdoing it. Your goal is simply to help a concerned person adopt a more creative attitude. Successful people are those who solve problems either by fixing malfunctions or by finding someone else who can.

◆ **Get agreements in writing.** Because every human being changes their views over time, request written agreements for all business transactions and make notes about what is said as well. In reviewing these documents, be alert to inaccurate information, but don't get paranoid—not everyone is as reliable as you would like them to be, including you!

◆ **Hold on to your dream.** Like a good detective, never stop searching until you find what you are looking for. Whether it exists in material form or in your imagination, it can be realized. In 1903, the Wright brothers made the first flight in history, traveling a distance of 125 feet—less than the length of a 747 jet. In 1969, Neil Armstrong walked on the moon. Over the course of only sixty-six years, human beings went from leaving the ground for the first time to walking on the moon, all because of a dream and the human capacity to turn dreams into realities. For the practical mystic, having dreams and finding ways to fulfill them is among life's most fascinating adventures.

◆ **Make every mountain into a molehill.** Some people speak in heavy, depressed tones of the many difficulties that stand between them and their goals. Certainly, the perception of such overwhelming obstacles is enough to deter 99 percent of all people from even attempting to realize their dreams. Instead of coming to fruition, their ideas would perch on a shelf to be brought down and admired from time to time, and then returned with regret.

Recognize that, yes, there is work to be done and bringing your dreams to fruition will take effort, but never see difficulties as obstacles to success. Giving up guarantees failure. When Henry Ford wanted to build an eight-cylinder engine out of one block, his engineers told him it was impossible. But he replied, "I want it, and I shall have it. Keep working until you succeed." And succeed they did, after much hard work.

Rather than becoming discouraged, acknowledge potential impediments and deal with them, no matter how long it may take. People who are successful in this world are those who face hurdles as challenges, thinking, "The sooner I get started, the sooner I will finish. This has to be done to achieve my goal, so I will do it." Such an attitude furthers the accomplishment of any goal, material or intangible.

Much of our reality is determined by our attitudes and outlook. If we see life as simple rather than difficult, it will become so. With this perspective alone we can conquer the vast majority of obstacles to success, for it leads to the realization that whatever problems arise can be solved. Our job, then, is to scale down the difficulties until they no longer look like Mount Everest. Yet even climbing a great mountain is a simple task; all it takes is walking. Manifesting our dreams begins with an optimistic attitude and a belief that problems can be overcome.

The Balance of Give and Take

Life is full of opposites. When it is day in our part of the world, it is night in another. Contrasts help us define our human experience. Had we never felt variations in temperature, for example, how would we perceive hot and cold? How would we appreciate pleasure were it not for pain? At a certain point we come to understand that phenomena exist *because* of their opposites; that black and white, hot and cold, good and bad all make each other possible; and that nothing is therefore truly good or bad. Once we realize that nothing is intrinsically good or bad but simply the polarity of its opposite, we discover how important it is to start viewing all phenomena objectively. When we see events as good or bad, on the other hand, we react emotionally, and more often than not, inappropriately—a tendency that can be understood as prejudice. In fact, "good and bad" is the basis for all prejudices.

With this in mind, consider whether you are creating obstacles to making money because of prejudices you may have. Ask yourself, for example, if something you have deemed undesirable could actually help you increase your income. When I was young, I decided never to be in the retail business, yet I ended up owning three retail stores, reaping a large profit from them each year, then selling them for enough money to be able to retire at a very young age. So it was that the one business I had rejected outright became the vehicle for my success. I compromised for eight years and in return gleaned sixty or seventy years of financial freedom—a very good deal. The moral of this story is that what appears distasteful from the lesser ego's perspective may in fact be highly advantageous.

Taoists say that from the opposites of yin and yang arose the "ten thousand things," meaning all things. To be peaceful, then, we must learn to balance opposites, especially the "give and take" in our lives. We give of our time and effort, and we take money that can help us do what we want, when we want. Upon finding a balance between give and take—although we often think we are giving more than taking because the "take" comes so much later—we achieve spiritual freedom and experience ourselves on a path of unity with the Tao or our god.

Maintaining a balance of give and take also applies to relationships. We may do whatever we can to help others, but when that entails significantly hurting ourselves or hindering our progress, it is time to refuse and begin practicing "constructive selfishness." Constructive selfishness should not be taken to an extreme, however, since the pleasure derived from helping others is often well worth the sacrifice involved.

Finding a balance between give and take is only possible when we realize that they are like the yin-yang symbol, shown above. Some circumstances involve more giving and less taking, then over time these dynamics reverse. While contemplating the overall balance of give and take in your life, you may therefore want to expand your view of time. If you live for eighty years, you may have to give unceasingly for the first forty, but then you'll get to take for the next forty. The incentive offered in the tiring period of giving is that you will receive with interest, resulting in a payoff worth ten times the investment. So it is important to learn to view give and take in terms of a long-term investment rather than only an immediate exchange.

Then, too, the yin-yang symbol has a spot of white in the black field, a spot of take in the give. Indeed, these two dynamics exist simultaneously as "yinyang," suggesting that you cannot give without getting. In offering a gift, you simultaneously receive pleasure. With this in mind, learn to feel the taking in the giving, and vice versa.

When I was in India, a friend offered to lend me a flute to take on my travels through the country. Since it was bamboo and therefore quite fragile, I had reservations and told him I was concerned about damaging it. "So take two," he replied. Worried about breakage, but understanding the joy in giving that my friend would feel, I took one flute—and didn't break it.

Money As a Tool

Money is to life what gasoline is to a car—the fuel that propels you to your destination. Whether we like it or not, we need it to reach our goals. Yet money in itself has no more power than we give it. In a sense, it is much like property, as is described in the following remark by a Sufi: "The world is God's property. If property falls into the hands of a dishonest man, it will be the cause of his downfall. If the property falls into the hands of a trustworthy man, it will become a means of honor and success. But the property in itself carries neither merit nor guilt. The merit or guilt is yours. Everything depends on how you use it."

Money, in other words, is simply a tool, as is all of God's "property." Depending on how we use it, it can either help us or lead to our undoing. Our role in relation to God's many gifts became clear to me the day I asked my Sufi teacher in Turkey about dangers of the logical mind overpowering the emotions. He replied, "God is perfect.

God does nothing other than what is needed and right. Everything that exists is from God, including functions of the mind. If he gave us a logical mind, we must use it in the same way we should use all his gifts." It was then I realized that our challenge is to use everything we are and have—all of God's gifts—as best we can, approaching our work and play with consciousness, compassion, and attention. In terms of the acquisition of money and the material things it can buy, this challenge is actually a spiritual exercise, for it forces us to use our gift of wise administration without becoming attached to anything, and in the process, to gain strength.

III. Psychological
And Emotional Refinement

Chapter 6

How to Deal With Desires

W e are ruled by our desires. While still unconscious, our desires are programmed—formed from the impressions left daily by TV commercials, billboard ads, and other visual and auditory messages—whereas when fully conscious we *choose* our desires. In progressing along the continuum from unconsciousness to consciousness, from asleep to awake, we participate more and more in the selection process. For example, at an early stage of waking up, an aspiring practical mystic will recognize animal desires but be unable to control them. At a later stage, he may notice these desires and actively resist them. Finally, as a practical mystic, he will be able to choose only those desires that empower his soul.

The Origin of Desires

It may be odd to think that acting on our desires can empower the soul, yet that is actually what happens once we have discarded our programmed desires. To see how this works, reflect on these four parts of our being: body, mind, heart, and soul. The *body* has needs and instincts. The *mind* reasons, but only to the degree that the heart and soul have developed control over it. The *heart* wants to love—anyone and everyone. The *soul* seeks truth about our reason for being and yearns to return to its source in full consciousness.

Although the soul is the core of our being, it is not in control. What most often rules is the body, the loudest and pushiest part of us. The body, however, is not a capable ruler, and as a result the other parts do not trust it enough to follow its commands faithfully, as you will see in exercise 6–1. The resulting dissension manifests in a quagmire of conflicting desires. Ultimately, the only way to become unified is for the soul, our place of connection with higher knowledge, to rule. If the soul is strong and the heart is pure, then together they can win over the mind. If the mind then joins with the heart and soul, the body can no longer get away with ruling like a spoiled child who always wants his way. When the mind and heart are united with the soul, desires are not denied or suppressed; instead, they *change*. Some disappear and new ones arise.

Exercise 6–1

Where Did This Desire Come From?

Any time you have a desire for something, or feel sad or lonely, ask yourself: "Who desires, who needs? Is it me or my body?" Once you know where the desire originates, decide whether or not its fulfillment will serve you. In this way you will learn to distinguish between the different parts of your being and their effect on you.

In someone who is still asleep, the body rules and the four parts perform the following functions:

> **Body** — Expresses demands
>
> **Mind** — Translates demands and acts
>
> **Heart** — Becomes clouded
>
> **Soul** — Is powerless to express itself

In someone who has awakened, the chain of command has reversed and appears as follows:

> **Soul** — Essence; provides connection to God
>
> **Heart** — Expresses essence through emotion;
> offers compassion and love
>
> **Mind** — Translates emotion into action
>
> **Body** — Carries out the mind's commands

Here the soul desires; the heart feels; the mind interprets the desires and feelings, and then commands the body to act on them. However, even though the mind and body think they are smart enough to know what the soul and heart really want, they are not. When they rule a sleeping person, they go crashing into brick walls and trees, getting lost and hurt because they are intent on fulfilling their own desires rather than obeying the soul. In the end, the part of us that is strongest determines who we are as a person and how we will live and interact with the world. This, then, is the reason for strengthening the soul.

With the soul in charge, we discover the truth of the saying "The more we know, the more we realize how little we know." While we are still ruled by the lesser ego, our modus operandi is more in keeping with "The less we know, the more we think we know." If we travel the world, we might discover how little we actually know about manners, food preferences, how to live in a straw hut or a high-rise apartment. If, however, we are familiar with only our small town and the information exchanged on the local street corner, we may think that our little niche of the world has taught us all there is to know. In much the same way, the soul is universal in its capacity to know all things, whereas the body's knowledge is limited to what it contacts directly with its sense organs. Thus, we live on one level of human existence if our soul is strong enough to rule, and on an altogether different level if our body rules.

To become unified under the soul's rule we must not only strengthen the soul but also call the other parts of our being into its service rather than allow them to run freely about. After all, a wise king can do nothing if he is tethered to his throne and has no servants in the castle to carry out his commands. Seen in other terms, once they are unified our four separate parts can work together to nourish us, whereas at a feast for the ego everyone leaves hungry. The following exercise can help you realign this chain of command.

Exercise 6–2

Redirecting Desires

Select a desire you currently have, then ask yourself, "Why do I want _____ [the object of a current desire]?" Question yourself deeply and sincerely. If your answer reveals that this yearning is not beneficial, redirect the desire to an object that will feed all parts of your being. Now choose another desire and repeat these two steps. Little by little your desires will become more harmonious with your true interests.

Types of Desires

Essentially, there are two types of desires: those of the world and those of a higher nature. Worldly desires are easy to recognize. They focus on possessions that are not necessary to our existence or that distract us from the emptiness we may occasionally experience. These desires emerge from the lesser ego and serve little useful purpose other than to numb our pain.

Desires of a higher nature, on the other hand, are useful to our development. They focus on objects or activities that push us toward personal growth or toward benefiting the world we live in. Actually, personal growth *is* for the benefit of the community, because as we develop we are better able to serve others. For instance, if you attend school for the sole purpose of self-improvement, your new skills will help you improve the lives of others. Desires of a higher nature emanate from a higher source, or intelligence, that communicates with us through our intuition. Ultimately, these desires can move us toward a balanced state in which we are no longer subject to the destructive pull of worldly desires.

When you have a clear understanding of the two types of desires, try to discern which of your longings are from a higher source and then focus your efforts on fulfilling them. As you do, remember that there is no need to suppress other desires. If a higher source gives you a desire for a type of work, for example, then it understands that you must earn money to live while fulfilling that desire. The fragmentation occurs not so much when we pursue worldly desires as when we *confuse* them with desires from the higher source and thus misdirect our focus and misuse our skills.

While learning to distinguish between the types of desires, we need to recognize two hidden realities: one is that because our lesser ego is so in control of our lives, we have lost touch with our intuition, and the other is that higher wisdom therefore strives to find its way to us through the vehicle of desire. Your job when faced with a desire, then, is to sort out whether it is a desire of the lesser ego or higher guidance disguised as a desire. It is simple to determine the difference—one is for toys, the other is for useful acts. All it takes is looking at what you really want and why. To practice, work with exercise 6–3.

Exercise 6–3

Which Type of Desire Is This?

To improve your ability to distinguish between types of desires, examine some of your past yearnings and see if you can tell which ones sprang from the lesser ego and which came from a higher source. If you do not wish to review the past, determine the source of your present desires. In either case, the best way to track a desire to its source is by looking at the outcome.

How, then, do desires eventually stop ruling us? Once you have begun to follow desires from a higher source, you will have fewer worldly desires. At that point you will have acquired the capacity to hear higher guidance through its natural channel of intuition. In time, the camouflaged vehicle of desire will no longer be needed to get information past the lesser ego, for desires will have given way to intuitional guidance.

Of course, none of these examinations takes place in a vacuum. In all our interactions with others, we need to see if what we are doing or asking of them is for a collective or purely personal benefit, be aware of how our motivations are affecting them, and be prepared to deal with the consequences of our actions. Awareness of how our desires influence others can provide a new lens for viewing our own troubles, further helping to change our lives.

How the Law of Opposites Presents Conflicting Desires

A Hindu painting shows good gods and evil demons fighting in a celestial war. The opposing forces are pulling on two ends of a rope attached to a butter churn. As they pull back and forth in their tug-of-war, the churn turns and out comes the Milky Way, our universe.

It is through this opposition of positive and negative, yin and yang, good and evil that all things come to exist. The entire universe is created by the never-ending movement of opposing forces. As energy generated by their movement flows outward, it accumulates in different places and grows into mountains or people or planets. Yet amid this natural flow of energy, nothing is destroyed; everything is merely transformed into a new creation.

A battery operates in much the same way. Two dissimilar metals with acid between them will, when placed next to each other, cause electrons to leave the metal with the weaker attractive force and migrate to the other metal—a dynamic known as the Volta effect. In the course of their migration, the free electrons travel through the acid to the positive and negative terminals, where they leave the battery and begin to furnish the attached device with electric current.

Like a battery's positive and negative terminals, the two opposing forces that create all movement are simply following the law of opposites. They have nothing to do with inherent good and evil, or positive and negative, and everything to do with human interpretation. Hence it is only our subjective view of reality that causes us to despair or lose motivation when things seem not to be going our way. By expanding our perspective, we would see that just as electrons subjected to opposing forces are not destroyed but only migrate to another medium, so do all the elements of our world. And each shift alters our life, as you will see while doing the following exercise.

Exercise 6-4

Watching Opposites at Work

*Observe how everything around you is created by opposition. As you do, notice the movement this causes, rather than concentrating on the apparent dissolution or destruction. In other words, focus on the **transformations** of matter instead of on the matter itself. Now bring this focus to your inner experiences and try to establish a perspective that frees you from feeling attacked or from thinking the world is out to get you. Understanding the many levels on which oppositional transformations occur will help you begin to direct the course of your life.*

Because we are subjected to opposing forces, we have conflicting desires. While experiencing the pushes and pulls of these desires, we may feel like a leaf blowing in the wind, or as though we were in a dark room with two people we cannot see, one on each side, spinning us around. If we could wake up and focus our attention, we would be able to choose which of the forces we wish to migrate toward. Then, by constantly reminding ourselves of the direction we want to move in, we can reduce the impact of conflict in our lives. We cannot eliminate the conflict of having two opposing desires, since such opposition is ever present in the material universe, but we can extinguish the conflict that arises over which one to select. With this issue resolved, our moods will brighten and our sleep requirements will decrease because our energy, no longer bound up in torment, will be creating more hours in a day.

Understanding Internal Conflict

Our difficulty with internal conflict comes from lack of under-standing. Although most of us want to feel safe, comfortable, and at peace, in our search to fulfill these desires we mistakenly look for a person to love, a new place to live, or a job that will make life more interesting. In other words, we search for solutions to internal con-flict outside of ourselves when the answers are *within* us. By waking up and unifying our fragmented self, we will find our essence, provider of enduring safety, comfort, and peace.

We humans are endowed with a small hunger and a greater hunger. The small hunger is for things of the world; the greater hunger is for food for the soul—specifically, finding the reason for our existence. Even when the small hunger is satisfied, the greater hunger will keep us in pursuit of something *more*. This is why a new partner, home, or job cannot on its own bring us the peace we are seeking.

It can, however, spur us on to work harder at waking up. We may feel content and relaxed with someone we love, but only for moments at a time, because there will soon arise a discomfort prompting us to continue our progress. Or we may feel relaxed with our partner yet a discomfort will develop in a different area, such as finances. In effect, it is impossible to simultaneously want growth and feel perfectly comfortable and relaxed.

Did you ever give up something only to find yourself *no* closer to a state of comfort? This can happen, too. When it does, knowing the *cause* of your discomfort can spare you needless agonies and fruitless quests. For example, if it is winter and the window is open, there is no point in turning up the heat—just close the window.

As you have probably guessed, most states of unrest are caused not by a material deficit but by wanting something of this world to satisfy a nonmaterial desire of the soul. The Hermetica, a 3,000-year-old body of teachings from the Middle East, puts it this way: Humans are part mortal and part immortal—both of which have needs and desires. If we are ignorant of the immortal part, we will try to satiate its hunger with food and physical pleasures, which cannot satisfy its needs. As a result, we will be perpetually unsatisfied and never understand why.

Paradoxically, we will attain peace once we have accepted conflict as the only possible state. We cannot feel steaming hot and ice cold at the same time, but we can experience the comforting warmth that comes when these opposites are in balance with each other. And we can always remember that yin is in yang, and yang is in yin, resulting in "yinyang." Since they must both exist simultaneously for the universe to function, conflict is the basis of life.

To further understand this universal duality, instead of calling it conflict you might prefer to envision a scale with each side keeping the other in perfect balance. One cannot exist without the other. Now, if you imagine temporary things of this world on one side of the scale and permanent spiritual truths on the other, you will see that such opposing desires cannot both be attained, and yet to exist, one requires the polarity provided by the other.

The streets of India offer an ongoing reminder of this coexistence of opposites. One man returns home in his chauffeured Rolls-Royce while another, who has no home and no possessions, leans against the building eating scraps of food that he shares with the birds.

Another helpful perception arises upon realizing that life, like the universe, is a never-ending circle. Accepting all opposites as simply facing points on this circle can change your vision of life and bring you closer to enlightenment, for you will be seeing positive growth rather than destructive loss. Even a building's demolition can be viewed as fertile ground for a new development. Seeing the new that will arise from ashes of the old is one sign of a mind in harmony with an ever-expanding consciousness of the universe. That is the mind of the practical mystic. The third force, the neutralizing circle that holds yin and yang, balances the polarities and, once understood, brings balance to life amid seeming chaos.

Building a Magnetic Center

By repeatedly focusing on a particular idea or desire, we build a magnetic center that will attract like phenomena. To attract the object of desire the magnetic center is built on, we must be consumed by that desire. This is a dangerous as well as beneficial practice, since such a center can attract destructive thoughts as easily as positive ones. For instance, we can build a magnetic center on self-destructive beliefs and defeat ourselves with low self-esteem. Yet as Taoists remind us, the Tao simply does. Hence it is up to *us* to determine if the thoughts we focus on are good or bad.

The influences that come our way are in large measure determined by the magnetic centers we develop within ourselves. For example, if we want material success, we would develop a magnetic center capable of bringing more opportunities for financial growth. If we are devoted to spiritual progress, we will develop a center capable of drawing to our attention inspiring literature or disciplines that will in turn attract higher influences. Of course, while seeking material success through a primary magnetic center, we can still attract spiritual influences through a less developed one, and vice versa.

The way we spend our focused time—the groups we belong to, the hobbies we pursue, the films we watch, and the literature we read—establishes the frequencies to which each of our magnetic centers is tuned. If we are interested in awakening and are spending time engaged in this pursuit, a magnetic center for it will draw influences of a high frequency our way. If instead we are immersing ourselves in superficial, mindless activities, we will attract lower-frequency influences that may keep us asleep.

Planting one stalk of corn in the middle of a field and watering it will not yield much to eat, yet will certainly spawn the growth of many weeds. We can live on weeds, but not as well as we can live on corn. So plant the food you desire all day, every day.

Chapter 7

Effective Communication

B ecause people around us do not necessarily think the same way we do, they cannot always understand our actions or motivations. Therefore, just as we must translate our words while speaking to someone from a different country, so must we find satisfactory ways of communicating to a person who has different aspirations or perspectives. The practical mystic, upon meeting another person, thinks, "I am a stranger in a strange land. I do not speak the language, and I must learn it if I want to get along successfully in this place."

If you have goals of evolving spiritually to benefit yourself and others, improved communication is essential. A life based on spiritual principles is certainly noble, yet it must be remembered that we live in a material world. Very often, people with spiritual goals cannot earn enough money to accommodate their own needs, much less assist others in meeting theirs. Frequently this is because the ancient principles of spiritually directed activity have not been explained in terms of financial prosperity. To adapt them to today's material realities, we must acknowledge that while a tree may be seen as a manifestation of God it is still a tree, and running head-on into it will hurt. Our primary concern must therefore be to deal with a tree as a tree; *then* we can remember who made it.

To gain a means of paying the bills accrued while accomplishing our goals, we must communicate in the language of this world, expressing our principles to others in ways that they can understand and relate to. We might try the Sufi approach of speaking on the student's level of understanding. Or we might instead strive to gently influence others by yielding to the flow of conversation, as is suggested in the following excerpt from Lao-tzu's *Tao Te Ching*:

> While living, one is yielding and receptive.
> Dying, they are rigid and inflexible.

All things, the grass and trees:
Living, they are yielding and forgiving;
Dying, they are dry and stiff.

Thus those who are stuck and inflexible
Resemble the dying.
Those who are yielding and open
Are in harmony with living.

Therefore an inflexible strategy will not succeed;
An inflexible tree will fall.
The position of the inflexible will not last;
The position of the yielding and open will advance.

To accomplish our goals in the world, we need not subscribe to the "fight, fight, fight" beliefs of society or compromise our ethics or principles. But we can still communicate effectively.

Words and Understanding

We speak with words and listen to them, but what are words? They are sounds that convey ideas. If I say the word *horse,* it may immediately conjure up in your mind an image of the animal we have come to know as a horse, but to someone who does not speak English the word will fail to bring this image to mind. Hence while either speaking or listening, it is of no use to get lost in words themselves; instead, we need to focus on the meanings *behind* them, on the ideas they are *conveying.*

Words are among the most dangerous powers a person can wield. When what we hear is not what the other person is trying to say—and conversely, when what we want to say is not what the other person is hearing—a conversation can quickly turn into a confrontation. The best precautions are first, not to take the words we hear literally, and second, not to trust our interpretations of others' statements. If you are in a bad mood and looking for trouble, you will interpret a sentence in one way, whereas if you are in a peaceful state of mind, your interpretation may be the opposite, resulting in an altogether different conversation. You alone are responsible for your reactions to the words of others. You can pick up a knife and stick it in your own heart or you can leave it on the table—the choice is yours.

My grandfather once told me a story that illustrates how easy it is to misinterpret words and respond inappropriately. After getting off the boat on his first visit to Morocco in 1920, he was approached by a local who made his living helping tourists. The man asked my grandfather if he needed a hotel. He did not, he replied. "Perhaps a nice woman?" the man continued. "Definitely not!" Then the man asked, "You want couscous?" My grandfather, ignorant of Moroccan cuisine, thought he was being cursed and replied, "Go to hell!"

The moral is this: Don't get lost in your interpretation of the words you hear, especially if you are not certain of their meaning or intent. Many arguments erupt because we interpret words according to what they mean to *us* rather than to the *speaker.* However, once you understand that words are nothing more than a series of sounds intended to transmit ideas, your perspective will quickly expand. You will discover that words are only the beginning—a means of opening the mind to receive a thought.

To bring this expanded perspective to the messages you convey, imagine that every word in your vocabulary has a thousand meanings. Accepting that your words will have different meanings to different people will greatly improve your ability to communicate without conflict. Remember, too, that while you are trying to communicate with someone who is in an upbeat frame of mind, they will interpret your statements in a positive light, whereas someone with a negative worldview will require clearer explanations. Everyone tends to interpret information in keeping with their present attitude toward life.

How to Improve Communication with Others

It is said that two minds working together can accomplish the work of four operating independently. Such harmony between people, even if only momentary, is a tremendous source of peace and joy. In fact, communicating free of power struggles is one of the most valuable skills we can possess, since it fosters the ability to succeed in business, have many friends, and most importantly, maintain a successful relationship with our partner and family. The art of helping people feel understood can change both their lives and ours. To succeed in mastering this art, we must sincerely try to be the most balanced, loving person we can be, remaining always at ground level, as the *Tao Te Ching* proposes:

> The rivers and seas draw all the streams
> Because they are skillful at staying below.
> Thus they are able to lead the streams to their goal.
>
> Therefore, to guide people wisely,
> One must lead humbly, staying below them.
> To remain a good leader of people,
> One must have support.
>
> Therefore evolved individuals remain in positions of leadership,
> And yet the people are not oppressed.
> They remain in front,
> And the people are not held back.
>
> Therefore the world willingly follows them,
> And does not reject them.
> Because evolved individuals do not compete,
> The world cannot compete with them.

Here are three simple suggestions for staying humble in your interpersonal relations:

1. **Ask, don't tell.** When assuming a position of authority, give orders only as a last resort. Harshly telling people what to do invites anger and resistance, which in turn will drain your energy and decrease your power; by contrast, asking people to do things helps them feel valued. Ask nicely, indicating your need. Working together, you will all be elevated.

2. **Don't blame.** Think twice about setting up boundaries to define your own tolerance levels and blaming others for crossing over them. Instead, strive to avoid being overly affected by others. If someone blames *you* for provoking *them,* examine whether or not you meant to hurt them. There is a big difference between a deliberately hurtful action and a person's inability to deal with life. Confident, successful people do not reproach someone with, "You really hurt me, and I need you to apologize." Rather, they are strong, not easily hurt, resilient, and willing to accept responsibility for the impact life has on them. They know this impact is associated with their own automatic reactions to events.

As much as possible, feel free to express yourself, unafraid that family and friends will reject you. To conserve energy and maintain equilibrium, strive to be unconcerned with others' opinions of you. There is no need to prove yourself to anyone as long as you yourself know who you are. The moment you give up trying to be perfect you will attain the emotional release needed to leap forward in your evolution, which will in turn enhance your social and business communications and help you gain emotional freedom.

Develop equanimity with the wisdom of a child. Remember the childhood adage "Sticks and stones may break my bones, but names can never harm me," and add, "unless I choose to let them."

3. **Don't argue.** Opposition from another person is likely to set the stage for conflict unless you think before speaking. Instead of reacting, take control of your lesser ego and assess what needs to be done. Arguing, on the other hand, is like fighting with a broken machine; it doesn't get anything to work. A conscious being responds to conflict with composure rather than reacting automatically and violently, as if suddenly awakening from a nightmare. To develop composure, work with the following exercise.

Exercise 7–1

Think before Speaking

To think before responding, practice speaking with an accent such as French or German. Expose yourself to the accent by watching a film or TV show, listening to a tape, taking a language class, or frequenting a cafe or restaurant that draws people from that country. Learn the intonations of the language so well that when you go to a store and speak with your new accent, others will believe you are really from that country. Even learn to mispronounce words or invert sentence structures as a citizen of that country might do. For instance, an East Indian might say: "I am going to be doing a most wonderful thing for you because you are being a most gracious person." This twisting of the tongue will force you to be conscious of the otherwise automatic function of speaking.

Discovering Root Causes of Behavior

To really understand what is going on with other people, we have to dig down to see what makes them "tick"—an activity to be applied to ourselves as well. Learning to see the root cause of a reaction takes practice, which we can do almost constantly without anybody knowing.

To determine the root cause of someone's behavior, ask questions rather than state facts. Questions will bring immediate feedback and help avert conflicts aroused by guessing. Remember, you are not trying to change the person; you are simply seeking to understand their point of view. Bavarians, in southern Germany, end their sentences with *or ?*—a custom that both allows that the speaker may be wrong and invites the listener to voice their opinion. You, too, may want to be careful not to impose your ideas on others. Finally, after finding the root cause of the person's actions, do everything possible to facilitate understanding and harmony.

When I worked as a mechanic for photo-finishing labs, the thirty-foot-long strips of paper would sometimes get stuck in the machine. If one got stuck near the back end of the machine, an adjustment often had to be made at the front end. Had I looked only at the spot where the paper got stuck, and not for the cause of the problem, I would never have been able to fix those machines.

This simple principle of looking for the root cause of problems can be used in a great variety of situations. As we know, most events have both a positive and a negative side, and it is only our perception that locks us into a certain viewpoint. For example, rain can ruin a picnic, yet at the same time trees need water to flourish. When we are able to see the good in the bad, we end up in balance. Once we start to dig for root causes and begin to hear the meaning behind words, we are no longer trapped in the limitations of language and no longer manipulated by our opinion of what a person meant by a particular facial expression or tone of voice. Then we will have gone beyond living on the surface of momentary experience to living within the meaning and essence of relationships.

Seeing Effects of Events through Time

For improved communication we also need to see that events have effects beyond the moment in which they occur. For instance, an event occurring now is actually influencing future circumstances. Upon understanding that what is happening now has far greater impact than is immediately evident, we open ourselves to the possibility of experiencing new dimensions.

In a sense, everything happening in this moment is like a stone thrown into a still lake. It is creating a disturbance, causing ripples that will travel outward in all directions—some on the surface and readily visible, others hidden below the surface. Far below, on the sandy lake bed, a disturbance with a rippling effect of its own will begin long after the stone's entry into the water. Present events, in other words, will affect us perceptibly and imperceptibly at various times in the future, and the greatest ramifications may occur in the distant future, in the form of new opportunities.

It is also true that whatever occurs now is related to something that happened in our past. Hence each present moment becomes an opportunity to heal the past in preparing for the future. Such work can happen only with our conscious effort and active participation. After all, we are the ones who determine if past events will continue to perturb us or will release their hold on us, as the following story reveals.

Two Zen monks, Koto and Hitashi, were walking together on a muddy road just after a heavy rainfall. They came upon a beautiful young girl dressed in a silk gown who wished to cross the road but didn't want to ruin her dress at the muddy intersection. Koto picked her up and carried her across, put her down on the other side, and bid her farewell.

Neither monk spoke until later that evening when Hitashi could no longer contain himself and angrily burst out, "How could you carry that lovely young woman? We are monks; we are not supposed to look at women, never mind touch them!"

Koto replied, "I left her at the roadside. Are you still carrying her?"

Seeing the more subtle effects of events through time requires an awake and balanced mind, because awakening and balance usher in clear insight. With clear insight comes the wisdom needed to avert or dissolve conflict.

Facing Conflict

Regardless of your efforts to circumvent conflict, at times you will be unable to avoid a confrontation. When faced with contention, you can learn a great deal about yourself and others by taking a number of steps:

1. **Realize that you and the other person are seeing the same thing differently.** As the disagreement takes form, gently give way and try to understand the other person. Letting go of the notion that you are better informed requires a willingness to humble yourself in order to achieve harmony.

2. **Attempt to see the situation from the other person's point of view.** Say, "I see your point. We are each approaching the situation from a different perspective, and that is the cause of this disagreement." Recognizing that you are coming from a place of understanding rather than attacking, the other person is likely to be more receptive. If so, the disagreement will probably end before brewing into a full-fledged argument.

3. **Slowly and gently express your point of view without antagonizing the other person.** Start with a small detail. Once that is digested, move on to another. If you push too hard and see fire in the other person's eyes, back off and change the subject, returning to it later to present your ideas in another way. A concept communicated gently and gradually can be accepted without argument. This step is somewhat like tackling a large pizza: you can't shove the whole thing in your mouth at once, but if you take one bite at a time you can slowly and pleasantly eat it all. Since the mind, like the mouth, rejects anything too large or disagreeable, it is important to be direct yet diplomatic in your presentation of ideas.

4. **Back down and apologize if you realize you are wrong.** Constant care must be taken to not let your lesser ego convince you that your opinion is the only right one. Listen with an open mind and heart to the other person's point of view.

In all aspects of life we must learn to be firm yet gentle. When facing conflict in particular, we must support our viewpoint as we would hold an egg—tightly enough not to drop it, but not so tight as to break it. The *Tao Te Ching* goes one step further by advocating that we yield in order to progress; by yielding to the forceful, we can eventually guide it onto a harmonious path, as is described in the excerpt on pages 99–100.

Yielding is also the principle underlying the Tai Chi exercise known as push hands. Here two people face each other, and one tries to push the other over. The person being pushed yields like a supple tree blowing in the wind, moving in such a way that the opponent rolls right off him. Once free of the attack, the one yielding allows his opponent to fall away and continues to move in his own chosen direction. When we are headed in a direction and something counters our movements, by yielding to the opposing force rather than confronting it head-on we can continue on our way.

We will always be faced with opposition of one sort or another, since that is the nature of our universe. The best solution is therefore to focus the mind on maintaining our direction so that when an opposing force appears, we will see it coming and be prepared to let it roll off us. The more developed the mind is, the more effective we will be in repelling attacks and surmounting obstruction.

Why should you be the one to yield rather than the other person? Because the one who yields, if willing to strive for self-improvement, is the one who grows in understanding and open-mindedness. Maturity, in this context, has nothing to do with physical age—a point parents need to keep in mind when using their age to end disputes with their children. Very young children, for their part, need to know that just because parents are older does not mean they are infallible. Idealizing a parent and then seeing them err can deeply confuse a child, often impairing trust later in life. However, if we raise our children to believe that parents make mistakes just as they do, and that we respect our children regardless of the age difference, they are likely to grow up with more self-assurance and respect.

Facing conflict with friends is no different. Here the point to keep in mind is that a friendship is often like a house of cards—built slowly through much effort, yet likely to collapse in an instant when one card is pulled out of place. To appreciate this dynamic, watch your response when a friend acts out of character. Do you get upset, or feel you no longer trust him? If so, make a mental note not to let your friendship be as fragile as a house of cards. Think before judging; question if you are actually right in your opinion and, when you are, if it is worth giving up the relationship. Also notice if you are guilty of similar faults. When you yield to others, consider the move an indication of your level of maturity—something not to flaunt but to use as a gauge in tracking your evolution.

Developing the Voice of Intuition

When we hear something new, it captivates our attention. When we hear something we've heard before, we tend not to listen as well because we think we already know about it. Even while searching for new ideas we often listen as if we were asleep—a phenomenon known as "sleep hearing." Consciously awakening the moment we hear an idea enables us to both absorb the information and benefit from the wake-up call.

This process also applies to ideas that spring from our intuition. When we get an intuitive thought about an event and fail to acknowledge it because it was unaccompanied by angels and heavenly music, we soon forget about the flash of awareness. But if an event we have foreseen suddenly happens and we remember the feeling of that premonition, we are more likely to pay attention to future premonitions.

For example, while leaving my house during a snowstorm one winter day, I had a vision of my car sliding down the road just in front of my destination. By the time I reached that road, I had forgotten about my premonition and failed to slow down. Only while sliding across a patch of ice to within inches of another car did I remember it—and quite vividly at that. Fortunately, we were able to avoid a collision, but had I paid attention to the intuitive warning, I would have avoided the near miss.

The more we remember that we once foresaw the future, and how that felt—which can be like anything from a physical twitch to a mental image—the more proficient we will become at receiving messages from our intuition and heeding our inner guidance. Such proficiency goes hand in hand with being present and awake at all times. For practice, work with exercise 7–2.

Exercise 7–2

Tuning into Intuition

To develop a link with your intuition, practice automatic writing. Sit quietly with pen and paper, or at your computer. Now jot down a question, contemplate it for a moment, then forget about it. Spend several minutes writing whatever comes to mind, without censoring or editing yourself. After a month of practicing this exercise for at least ten minutes two or three times a week, begin to pay attention to the thoughts that arise following your writing session. Are you having insights into matters you know nothing about? For a variation on this exercise, sit quietly and write whatever comes to mind without first asking a question.

To gain full value from this practice, keep it going for several months. Before long, you should be feeling your intuition more and more strongly.

The practical mystic, whose mind is free of preconceived ideas, is able to intuit not only personally relevant information butalso other people's thoughts and feelings. To see how this works, try it with people you know very little about, for then your mind will be clear of subjective opinions and open to thoughts from their mind. Never use your intuitive insights for purposes of showing off, however, since this would strengthen your lesser ego and work against your own development. Instead, just quietly observe the flow of information coming your way.

Once you have established a reliable link with your intuition, you can give it a "voice" and let it "speak" to you. Communication from your intuition will then serve as a trustworthy form of inner guidance. To get started, work with exercise 7–3.

Exercise 7–3

Developing Clear Inner Guidance

To give your intuition a voice, think of someone, either dead or alive, whom you regard as a source of wisdom. Then develop a mental relationship with that person, calling upon them whenever you wish, not only for help but also for companionship. Each time you talk to each other, believe that your invisible friend is with you. Have a real conversation with them, letting your mind accept any thoughts that arise.

If you repeat exercise 7–3 frequently, always thinking of the same person, they will become the focal point of your efforts. In time their image may become more vivid or, to the contrary, disappear entirely; in either case, your intuition will have developed a strong voice of its own. When you sense the strength of its voice, consider adding another person to your talks, eventually gathering together a *group* of people, each of whom possesses a character trait you admire and wish to have. Think of these people as your advisers, and do not be overly concerned if they begin to feel present and your conversations with them seem realistic. Some of your advisers may even appear in your dreams, which Sufis and Kabbalists view as vehicles for communicating with intuition. Be sure to keep a journal of this counsel for future reference.

To nurture your voice of intuition, practice listening for it. Because answers to your questions will seem like normal thoughts, you may initially discredit them. Indeed, some answers will emerge from your lesser ego, yet others will not. The difference will be evident when you get a thought you never had before or an answer you did not know. Use this method to validate that intuition is in fact the source of the thought. To check for accuracy, see how future events turn out.

Both these methods have proved invaluable to me. Once, while sitting alone in meditation, I heard a voice, as if from another person in the room, say, "Church of a Thousand Names, Cyprus." Having never heard of Cyprus before, I was surprised when about two weeks later a friend mentioned a book about a spiritual teacher in Cyprus whom I might be interested in meeting. I then asked a professor of mysticism about the message I'd heard, whereupon he explained that "Church of a Thousand Names" is a Sufi term. Spurred on by these two events, I eventually went to Cyprus. There, at the school presided over by the teacher my friend had mentioned, I met someone who led me to a Sufi order in Istanbul—something I had been searching for throughout the previous decade.

Another time, while alone in a small chapel in England, I heard a clear voice recite six numbers and the words "Three weeks." Three weeks later, I purchased a lottery ticket with those six numbers, only to find that they were each one digit away from the winning number. I concluded that although we receive accurate messages from our intuition, if it is not our destiny for a particular event to happen, it won't; if what we wish for could in any way hurt us, it will not be granted; and if we misuse our abilities, they will not function correctly. Of equal importance, I was shown that something invisible was real and that its guidance could be relied on as long as the timing was best for all concerned.

Some people who establish an intimate connection with their intuition later lose trust in it. If this has been your experience, examine why you lost faith in this aspect of yourself. Did other people criticize you for following your inner guidance? Did you have trouble distinguishing the voice of intuition from the demands of the lesser ego? Once you know the root cause for the disconnection, work to redevelop trust in your intuition.

Reopening this channel of communication may entail nothing more than conversing with your intuition through automatic writing or meditation. The former approach will be highly effective if it is easier for your hand to flow freely than for your cynical mind to trust the thoughts it receives.

Chapter 8

Managing the
Emotions

As the eyes are windows to the soul, the emotions are doors that let in—or keep out—growth-promoting experiences. Soul growth *depends* on emotional experiences; living without them withholds nutrients from the soul. However, while we are asleep, the logical and calculating conscious mind barricades the doors of emotion like a suit of armor, deflecting emotional content from its course to the soul.

As Westerners, we are primarily intellectual beings who use the mind to interpret and transmit emotional experiences. But we cannot feel our emotions by thinking about them. Instead, we must let them arise on their own, independent of the mind's invented agendas and interpretations. For instance, if you have a psychic experience such as a vision of God, and think, "I am seeing God," the experience will immediately dissipate. The logical mind, invested with the job of keeping the body safe, limits its scope of activity to the gross material dimension. Hence being informed by the logical mind is like watching a river of feelings; we can see the flow of water but cannot follow the individual drops, since they move too quickly to be tracked by the intellect. So absorbed are we in accepting only what fits our intellectual image of ourselves that we fail to participate in the exceptional, more fleeting events that enrich the quality of our experience.

For emotional content to reach the soul, we must work from the innermost sanctum of our being, which can be reached in most cases by unsealing the armor of the mind. Shut tight, the mind strongly resists the penetration of new material; open, it allows experiences to flow effortlessly in and out. By contrast, if we try to open the heart directly, an uncontrollable experience may scare us into an even deeper shutdown, or simply evoke feelings of emptiness.

To visualize this predicament, imagine standing in the center of a castle that is built around your essence, with all the doors locked and barred. Part of you is outside trying to get back in so that you can achieve wholeness again. To enter the castle on its own, this part would have to either break down one of the doors or blast through it with explosives, resulting in a pile of rubble. It would also lead to extensive damage, because on the other side of the newly demolished door lies a sensitive heart, unprotected and unprepared to deal with the world as it really is. Forcing open the vulnerable heart in this way is sure to provoke an overemotional, overreactive state in which the simplest needs in life would appear too enormous to address. As a Sufi teaching puts it, "It is not up to you to open your heart. God alone knows when you are ready. At that time, he will open it for you."

However, if the locked-out part of you were to enter the castle through a carefully unlatched door, it would be able to reach the interior and achieve wholeness. You would then have the ability to consciously open or close any door as needed from within, rather like installing and removing the filters referred to on page 25. To gently prepare the emotional center for this opening, practice exercise 8–1.

Exercise 8–1

Gently Opening the Heart

To begin to open the emotional center, relax and place your attention on the area of your solar plexus, just above your belly button. Sense the physical feelings that are arising there. Practice this exercise for at least ten minutes a day.

To appreciate the challenges involved in accessing your essence, imagine it trapped within a castle whose many doors except for one are guarded by little I's; here the law of the land dictates that one door must always be open and unguarded. As the part of you that is seeking to return approaches the open door, one of the I's sees you coming and, leaving his post, shuts the door. Noticing the now open door at his previous post, you run toward it. But again a guard sees you and shuts the door before you arrive. The way out of this dilemma is by doing as many of these exercises as often as possible, for with each one that you practice on a regular basis, you will be placing a little angel outside a door of the castle. Once there are angels posted at all the doors, including the unguarded one, you will be able to enter. This entry into the castle will mark the moment of encountering your essence, the soul. And with the arrival of the missing part of you comes a growth-promoting experience.

Identification and Moods

One of the ways in which the flow of emotions is deflected from the soul is through identification, or losing ourselves in an object of thought, which ends up dictating our moods. The process begins when we mindlessly identify with some aspect of our environment, allowing its stimuli to control our thoughts and feelings. Just as the lungs breathe in and out and the heart beats, so does the mind feed constantly on the impressions it receives; hence in identifying with an external reality, we lose our mind to our surroundings. When we are *not* identified with things around us, we are free to choose how we want to feel, but for that we must be awake.

One day several years ago, I happily boarded a train for a long trip from Spain to Rome. As the day went on, we rode through one run-down village after another until I, too, began to feel run-down. Then about five hours later I looked out the window and saw that we were traveling along the Mediterranean, where people were playing on the beaches and enjoying the sun and sea. Instantly, I felt wonderful. This is a classic example of identification. At first, I identified with people in the slums and felt as depressed as their surroundings looked. Then when the scene changed to reveal a beautiful landscape and happy people, my mood lifted.

We easily identify with events and people around us. For instance, have you ever felt suddenly tired after spending time with someone who was incessantly complaining? Through self-observation, we can see how our moods are constantly manipulated by our false self, which loves to identify. Each time we become conscious of this tendency, we decrease the likelihood of its happening again under similar circumstances. As unattached observers of life, we can eventually be who we really are rather than what we identify with. In this way, we can learn to react appropriately to both business and personal situations.

If someone is in pain, for example, we can either become trapped in their suffering, and thus become ineffective, or offer the solace of compassion. Offering compassion is not so much a matter of extending love to another person or feeling sorry for them as it is *understanding* their pain. Feeling the other person's pain without being sucked into their whirlpool of self-pity keeps us strong and solid enough to provide a comfortable, safe setting in which they can relax and ease their agony.

To free yourself from identifying with the emotions of others, and to refine your capacity to be truly helpful, attempt to view all of life objectively. See the events of each day as if you were standing on top of the Empire State Building looking down at little ants busily running about. Then envision yourself as one of these ants, all the while remembering that in this awakened state you can choose the emotions that will course through you rather than be chosen by them. Identifying with an emotion is akin to being lost in a maze, whereas viewing the situation objectively gives you a chance to look down on it from above and choose your path.

Fear

We also hamper our soul growth by identifying with our fears. Since many fears are programmed thought forms that we have acquired, we can rid ourselves of them through the same power that created them—namely, conscious focused thought. A good way to do this is to deliberately place ourselves in a situation that ordinarily arouses fear, and then talk to ourselves as if we were another person wondering where this fear began. We might also tell ourselves that there really is nothing to be scared of, that many people are holding up quite well under similar circumstances, and that we are sure to emerge safely. This method of objectively analyzing a dreaded situation, rather than identifying with a programmed response to it, allows us to confront it head-on, and is therefore highly effective in conquering fear. After all, there is actually nothing to fear but fear itself.

While living in Osaka, Japan, for example, I dealt with my fear of being alone in the following way. Every weekday at about 5:00 in the afternoon I would go watch people meeting their friends at the train station after work. How happy they looked as they went off in pairs or groups to spend the evening together! Eventually, I would be standing there alone. Of course, I felt very sad knowing that all these people were going to be with their friends while I would be by myself. However, the more I deliberately faced my fear, the less it devastated me. Soon I was able to notice fear rising up in me at other times, too. But feeling it coming, I was better able to cope with it. After a few weeks of self-imposed suffering, I unearthed the root cause of my fear of solitude, at which point I became free of it.

The reason fear is so powerful is that we are not conscious of its presence until it is well entrenched in our minds. In fact, ignorance keeps us trapped in an endless circle of fears until we acquire the knowledge that can wash it away, as I was to rediscover upon returning from my travels. I had long been terrified of knives, then one day while visiting my mother, I experienced a flash of insight. As she was washing the dishes, she mentioned that she had always been scared of knives. My fear vanished instantly, for in my long-practiced state of wakefulness I was able to see the connection between my mother's fear and my own. It was as if I were suddenly present enough to enter my being through a newly opened door and discard a fear that was mine only by association.

There are also irrational fears to deal with. When I was learning to fly small airplanes, the first time I approached a solitary puffy cloud, my body began to tense up with fear. My eyes reported that I was about to fly into a solid object, no matter how convincingly logic announced it was only mist. The closer I came to the cloud, the more my body stiffened. Finally, I sailed into and out of the cloud—an act that on its own banished the fear. Since then, I have flown effortlessly through many clouds. Knowledge alone cannot help us master these irrational fears, since although the intellect may know there is no cause for panic the body seems to have a mind of its own. Our only course is to carry on and let direct experience prove the truth of certainty.

Significant progress in life hinges on willpower, which is developed by confronting fears and dislikes—the rational as well as the irrational ones. Convincing ourselves that these are signs of impending danger when they are not will only further debilitate us. Instead, we must learn to face them one by one, continually reminding ourselves that we succeeded before and will again. The following story illustrates how conquering fear can lead to increased willpower, freedom, and welcome transformations.

A very long time ago, there was a young servant boy named Habibi, who was a kind and gentle soul. From the time of his birth, he had a peaceful nature that led him to do whatever was asked of him. He never questioned his tasks or considered a job too menial for him. He contentedly served his masters and felt great joy in knowing he was helping to increase the happiness in people's lives.

One day, Habibi was traveling with his master's family when they were attacked by pirates. The pirates killed the entire party, one by one, until they came to Habibi. He was standing there peacefully, not yelling in fear, not even quivering before his inexorable fate. Curious, the pirate leader spoke to Habibi: "You have seen how I treat prisoners, yet you do not show fear of your inevitable death. This fascinates me. I think I will spare your life today. Perhaps I will kill you tomorrow."

Habibi reacted as he did to all things—with calm acceptance, for he knew there was nothing more to life than to do what was in front of him and to love without fear. He also knew that death was inescapable and that each day brought a new world with new people. After all, one day he had been living in luxury with a loving master and now he was a slave to pirates, eating scraps off the floor. Tomorrow, he thought, may bring yet another world. Habibi believed that each day must be lived with all his heart, as if he were serving God, for God had created both the loving master and the pirates.

For days, Habibi worked with all his heart despite the harsh treatment he received. He lived by doing for the sake of doing, and not for a reward. Each night before retiring, the pirate leader came to him and said, "You did a good job today. I will spare your life. Perhaps I will kill you tomorrow." Weeks passed, then years, and each night without fail, the pirate leader came to him with the same message.

Habibi stayed on with the pirates and grew into a fine young man. One day, the aging pirate leader called Habibi to his cabin. "Habibi," he said, "I am aging, and this pirate business is very tiring for an old man. I have enough wealth to live out the rest of my days with no concerns, but I have become a legend and would like that to continue. You have proven to be a man with a will stronger than any I have seen. Would you like to take my place?"

Habibi agreed. Since he knew the pirate better than anyone else, having served him all these years, Habibi easily took over the position. But because his heart had never hardened despite all the torture and murder he had seen, he made a few changes in protocol. Under his leadership, the pirates patrolled the waters and protected innocent travelers, helped those in need, and ensured that the old pirate would go down in history as a kind protector of the seas.

The most important task for achieving balance and harmony, as well as spiritual growth and success, is the conquering of all fears, for with that comes freedom. In fact, fear and freedom are two sides of the same coin. When one is visible, the other cannot be seen.

While paralyzed by fear, we cannot experience the fullness of life. We are left with only a limited range of emotions and precious few moments of trusting. Moreover, we begin to confine our experiences to the familiar, restricting the number of sensory impressions that nourish the mind. For example, some people are not willing to travel to the Far East because the plane might crash, or they might get a disease and die, or they cannot bear to see poverty for fear that they, too, may end up impoverished. Not only does fear stop us from living, but it keeps us physically tense, waiting for the moment when the dreaded object or situation might appear.

The way to conquer fear is to do what you are scared of doing—at every possible opportunity. When you have conquered a fear in one instance, remember that you have succeeded, for this will help you gain strength the next time you face a similar terror. Another aid in alleviating fear is research. If you have a fear of flying, for instance, find out the annual percentage of plane flights worldwide that result in a crash, then calculate your odds of dying in such a wreck.

Of course, extraordinary events, both negative and positive, do occur, but they happen so infrequently that it is useless, if not devaluing, to live in fear of them. In one such instance, an individual was driving on a mountain road when a boulder landed on his car and killed him—the first time an event of this nature had taken place since the building of the road decades before. This was such a strange occurrence that it would not even be a thought for most people. Disasters happen so unpredictably and in such strange ways that if fate is behind them the inevitable will happen regardless of what you do to protect your safety.

Another extraordinary event, one with a happier ending, involved the mechanic who restored my first airplane—a man who had been flying for twenty-five years with a perfect record. When he had finished working on my plane and taken it on a test flight, he got about 400 feet off the ground, made an error, and came straight down, crashing into a stand of trees. The plane was demolished, but the mechanic miraculously walked away with only minor cuts and bruises. Even more miraculous than his survival is the fact that while over the previous ten years he had been in severe back pain and had been living on painkillers in spite of three back operations, after the crash his back problems disappeared.

These true stories illustrate how useless it would be to plan your life hoping for a miracle or fearing a disaster. Like the boulder falling from the mountain, some things just happen, and in the case of the plane crash, they happened for the best. The following Sufi tale shows the irony of trying to control destiny.

A man saw the Angel of Death in a marketplace and did not like the way Death looked at him. Immediately, he went to his boss, the mayor of the village, and asked for his fastest horse so he could go to Baghdad and hide from Death. His request was granted, and off he went.

Meanwhile Death, being a respectful sort, paid the mayor a visit. The mayor asked Death why he had looked so strangely at his employee upon seeing him in the marketplace. Death replied, "It was just that I was so sur-prised to find him here. You see, I have an appointment with him tonight in Baghdad."

From this perspective it becomes clear that living in a prison of fear prohibits us from experiencing life. If we fear rejection, we may be too frightened to enter into an intimate relationship or apply for a better job. If we fear good-byes, we may never say hello. Living begins when fear ends.

Anger

Anger, like fear, is a strong emotion we may easily identify with. The true source of our anger is often removed from the object of its attack; angry at a computer, for example, we may yell at a coworker. But if we develop the habit of differentiating between the *real* cause and the *apparent* cause, we will not vent our anger at the innocent. Just as turning on the light in a dark room lets a child know there is no monster about, so can a ray of objectivity help us see beyond the apparent cause of our anger to the real culprit.

There are three ways to deal with anger—to vent it, to repress it, and to let it dissolve. The first two strategies cause destruction: venting anger can end up hurting someone else, and containing anger is analogous to keeping a cobra in your house where it can eventu-ally attack *you.* The third strategy, letting anger dissolve, is akin to putting a cup of water out in the hot sun where it can evaporate—a safe and healthy option.

Until you learn to dissolve your anger, you can take measures to moderate it. To mitigate the negative consequences of vented anger, distinguish between real and apparent causes by observing your actions as soon as possible after an outburst. When approached sin-cerely, self-observation and apologies to people harmed often dispel the darkness cast by misguided rage. It can take time to see beyond illusions, so be patient and persistent.

To reduce the frequency of angry outbursts, see if the real cause of your anger is worth all the upset. It wastes energy to get angry at something that is irrelevant and will soon pass. It's like grumbling about rainy weather when you know your happiness will be restored just as soon as the sun comes out. Anger, like grumbling, doesn't help.

Repressed anger must be averted or it will build to volcanic proportions. Shundar, a Nepalese friend who travels extensively in Western countries, once remarked on how differently anger is handled in Nepal. He pointed out that when couples in the West get upset they keep their agitation inside; there the little disturbances accumulate until one day a minor mishap sets off a big fight that ends in irreparable damage and possibly divorce. By contrast, Shundar and his wife immediately express their anger to the responsible agent, which is not necessarily their spouse; when it is, they yell and scream, break a dish, then after the storm blows over, they love each other again. Because they refuse to keep their agitation inside, minor incidents do not grow into big problems.

Anger can be either destructive or constructive, depending on whether it is *at* or *for* something. Anger *at* is destructive and serves no useful purpose. It is the emotion we express toward drivers who cut us off. This type of anger robs the growth process of vital energy and can become addictive, like misery. A friend and teacher once told me, "Some people love their suffering so much I don't have the heart to take it away from them." Anger *at* is consuming. Like a wildfire with more and more forest to decimate, it continually replenishes its force, rarely burning itself out. If it is not dissolved, it simmers down, laying in wait for yet another reason to control your mind and have you blow up at a mere trifle.

Anger *for*, on the other hand, is a positive force that many highly successful people use to significant advantage, directing it rather than letting it consume them. Anger *for* is the type of anger we have about injustice, poverty, or educational, socioeconomic, health, or racial inequities—phenomena beyond our control that limit people from expressing their full potential. It makes us want to constructively change the way things are.

Anger *for* the improvement of life often provides the passion that fuels success, like the fire that heats the water for running a steam engine. Mahatma Gandhi, feeling anger for the British injustices toward the people of India, once said, "I have learnt through bitter experience the one supreme lesson: to conserve my anger, and as heat conserved is transmuted into energy, even so our anger controlled [focused] can be transmuted into a power which can move the world." And move the world he did! Gandhi's passion was so fervent that 250 million people supported his cause, ultimately returning the control of India to India.

Like Gandhi, be angry if you live in limitation, be angry if you are restricted—and let your anger fuel an effort to overcome the constraints. In the process of constructively releasing your indignation, you will boost your vital energy rather than swell like a can of soda that's about to explode.

Always question whether you are angry *at* or angry *for*. If you do not know, look for physical cues: anger *at* feels like your body is tensing up, or like you can't breathe, or like a gremlin is eating you from the inside, whereas anger *for* feels more like you are being propelled from the inside. Once you have identified the type of anger you are feeling, recognize that anger *at* someone must be dissolved and anger *for* an injustice can be expressed, then take the appropriate measures.

Dissolve anger *at* through self-observation. Begin by tracing the anger to its root cause, much as you would search out the origin of a thought, as described in exercise 2–3 on page 22. If you find that the cause of the anger does not merit an outburst, chances are the rage will quickly dissolve on its own. If it does not, you may safely assume that the lesser ego has taken charge. Because it does not want you to look like a fool for blowing up in public over something ridiculous, it has you justifying your angry reaction, and staying angry.

The cure for harboring useless anger is to learn to laugh at the foolishness of your pointless actions. Once you can see that you, like the buffoon in a slapstick movie, have slipped on the proverbial banana peel, the anger will vanish, since you cannot laugh and be angry at the same time. Self-directed humor is a long-term remedy, for those who can laugh at themselves will never cease to be amused.

The Dalai Lama, exiled leader of Tibet, knows the value of not harboring anger. A reporter once asked him how, after all he had been through—the massacre of his people, the invasion and occupation of his country, the destruction of its history and culture—he maintained his positive attitude. The Dalai Lama replied, "Do you have a better alternative?"

Imagine what your business and personal relationships would be like if you never got needlessly angry. Then next time you are in a frustrating situation, aware that exploding will only make it worse, think of this story:

When I was in India, I quickly learned that getting a train ticket there is an experience unlike any in the West. The normal procedure is to push your way to the ticket booth, along with twenty or more other travelers, all clutching their money and attempting to thrust it at the ticketseller. Whoever's money he takes gets the next ticket. This is not the place for a polite, wait-your-turn type of person.

Aware of the chaos, I went a day early to buy a ticket to Alleppy and was delighted to find the station relatively uncrowded. "Is there a train going to Alleppy tomorrow morning?" I asked the attendant.

"Yes sir, there is a train going there every day."

"Are you sure there is a train going tomorrow?"

"Yes sir, certainly. There is a train going tomorrow morning— nine o'clock."

"Good, can I reserve a seat on that train?"

"No sir, there is no reserved seating. You come tomorrow and get ticket."

"I would like to be sure of getting a seat. Can I please have a ticket?"

"No sir, no need to reserve. There are many seats every day on this train."

After a few more pointless attempts to secure a seat for myself, I finally gave up and left, hoping for the best. The next morning the same attendant was at the ticket booth. When I requested a ticket to Alleppy, he replied, "Sorry sir, there is no train going there today." "What do you mean there is no train. Yesterday you said there would be a train today."

"Yes sir, I said there would be a train today."

"Well then, I'd like a ticket."

"No sir, there is never a train going there this day."

"But you said there is a train every day."

"Yes, I said there is a train every day, but there is no train today. There is never a train this day."

With steam rising in me, I screamed, "If there is no train going today, why did you tell me there would be one?"

The attendant looked me straight in the eyes and said, "I did not want to get you upset."

Depression

Depression, which is partly anger at oneself, is self-destructive and a huge energy drain, often leaving the person unable to function even minimally. An illness of the will, depression can be so debilitating and the will so diseased that friends and loved ones are frequently prompted to offer encouragement. But telling a depressed person to take control of themselves and stop wallowing in self-pity is like telling a kindergartner to solve a nuclear physics problem—not very effective.

Different types of depression will respond for varying amounts of time to different catalysts. For example, a mental or emotional depression caused by loneliness may be temporarily alleviated by finding a new job or falling in love. Such a cure will be more enduring if the problem is on the surface of the personality. If the person is more subtly affected—lacking a sense of purpose, for instance—a deeper exploration may be required.

A basic spiritual and psychological premise is that gifted people will suffer psychologically when their gifts are not used to the utmost. The truth is that such suffering is not limited to those we refer to as gifted, but extends to all humans, since we are all gifted in one way or another. And just as the full moon outshines the light of the stars, so do people with flamboyant lifestyles occasionally cause those with smaller lights to fade into the darkness. When one of those little lights becomes dimmed by feelings of inferiority, depression may ensue. So it is that we all have something to offer, and when we fail to "radiate" it we suffocate the bit of God in us that wants to express itself, even if that bit of God wants nothing more than to be an excellent mail carrier.

Humans, unlike other creatures, are part mortal and part immortal. The immortal part wishes to reveal itself, to manifest that attribute of God it is destined to be. In failing to express our talents, whatever they may be, we prevent that immortal part of us from living as it wishes to—and thus squelched, it causes depression. In this sense, creativity is both a blessing and a potential curse, for with it comes the mandate "Use me or else . . ."

Viewed in other terms, the mind has to "breathe," inhaling thoughts to contemplate and exhaling ideas. Contemplating the inhaled thoughts creates the ideas, which rely on human talents for their expression. Ideas that are not expressed become very unhappy, because they want to go outside to play so they can mix with new thoughts. If our ideas cannot go outside to play, their unhappiness becomes our depression.

The Talmud addresses this point in a story about Rabbi Yochanan and Resh Lakish, the disciple and colleague who asked him the most difficult questions. When Resh Lakish died, Rabbi Yochanan went into a terrible depression—worse than any he had experienced, even after the death of his young children. His deep depression was attributed to the sudden loss of intellectual and spiritual stimulation in his life.

If you are depressed and wondering why, ask yourself the following questions: "Am I expressing my creativity? Am I using my mind to think about, learn, and share subjects that interest me? Am I useful to someone on a daily basis, even if it is a different person each day?" (*Note*: Do not save these queries for a major depression. A light perpetual unrest is also not something you need to live with.) If the answer to any of these questions is no, do what you can to change it. For starters, realize that when you are depressed your eyes are cast downward and you are unable to see the help that is in front of you. So raise your eyes and look around at life's opportunities—and your spirit may follow.

Depression can have even more subtle causes than an unacknowledged sense of purpose or unexpressed innate abilities. For example, science has substantiated that the physical body is electrical in nature and that the brain functions by receiving and transmitting electrical impulses. Eastern teachings tell us about the electrical field of the aura and chakras, or energy centers that determine levels of physical and spiritual functioning; the Kabbalah and Sufism describe similar energy centers. Our bodies, like everything else in the universe, are each vibrating at a frequency of their own. Hence living or working in an environment with a very strong electrical charge or sound vibration that does not resonate with our own can produce a state of mental or physical unrest.

The first step in assisting someone out of depression of any sort is to support them in striving to help themselves. If self-help proves to be beyond their capacity because of the depth of the depression, other action can be taken through the aid of a competent physician, counselor, or healer. When reaching out, vigilance is advised, since little has changed since the Hermetica, a philosophical text over 3,000 years old, warned its readers to beware of the many false teachers in their midst. In addition to advocating for self-help or assistance from the healing community, it may also be possible to remove the depressed person from inharmonious environmental frequencies, although relocation will require effort on their part and an unpredictable period of time before yielding results.

Regardless of the method used to lift a person out of depression, there is always a chance of relapse if they are repeatedly exposed to the same precipitating circumstances. To avoid a recurring depression, the person may need to strengthen and educate themselves enough to counteract regressive tendencies. A good preventive measure would be to learn about the body's electromagnetic field and how it is affected by emotional trauma, physical shock, or purely energetic influences.

Recently, while driving with a friend, I explained a vision I'd had of building retreat centers where people could take a few months' or year-long sabbatical to cure themselves of depression and live as practical mystics *without* the distractions of everyday life. "Do you think you can really transform a person that dramatically in a few months?" she asked. At that moment a car pulled in front of us bearing the answer to her question on its custom license plate: "U CAN."

Stress

Although a person with a highly stressful job is deemed worthy of respect in today's society, stress itself causes many illnesses. It is also an acceptable excuse for rude or improper behavior. Ironically, we have elevated stress to such grandiose heights that, despite its known consequences, it is at best an enviable state and at worst a dangerous cover-up.

Consider the response you might elicit by telling a coworker or partner that you are under enormous stress. You are apt to be greeted with compassion, understanding, even admiration. Now, what might happen if instead you had said you were depressed? More than likely, it would be heard as a complaint and received with pity or immediate retreat. Curiously, the precursor to being stressed often turns out to be a depression that has not been expressed because of society's negative image of this emotional state. Spiced up as stress, depression often remains unacknowledged, untreated, and as a result, increasingly crippling.

For this reason it is wise to seek out the root cause of any stress you are experiencing. Are certain demands on your time or energy causing undue pressure? If so, make appropriate changes and see if they lead to a reduction in stress. If they do not, go deeper into the heart of the problem. Are you feeling despondent because some aspect of your existence is unfulfilling, or because you do not know your purpose in life? If so, accept that the problem is not stress but depression, and that denial of the depression is the root cause of the trouble. Then address the depression, mustering whatever courage you will need to turn it around.

Insecurity

Many of us are scared to make decisions for ourselves. Our insecurity stems from a fear of taking responsibility for the consequences of our actions. To carry on, we let *others* make decisions for us, figuring that any unwanted outcomes will then be their fault. At such times, we are doubly accountable—responsible not only for the outcome but also for having turned over our decision making to someone who has no knowledge of our essence.

When we were young, our parents decided what we should wear, eat, and play, believing they were acting in our best interests. Now that we are able to take care of ourselves, there is no purpose in letting others make our choices for us. Waking up and breaking free of these habits of dependency can bring us abiding confidence in *ourselves*.

Finding the cause for our lack of self-confidence in decision making is less important than correcting it, which can be accomplished by simply taking charge of ourselves. Step one in taking charge is to accept that we must make all personal decisions on our own. Certainly we may learn a great deal from helpful advice, but the responsibility for determining our path in life, and all that goes with it, is ours alone. Step two is to accept that we will make some wrong decisions along the way, since errors occur in *any* learning process. Step three is to realize that anyone can make these mistakes, and that unless we have a direct telephone line to God the odds are most in our favor if we rely on ourselves.

Practice will increase the number of correct decisions we make, which will in turn increase our self-confidence and self-esteem. While practicing, however, we need to keep reminding ourselves that mistakes are normal. Remember, good judgment comes from experience, and experience comes from bad judgment.

In seeking counsel from others, we must therefore be sure to exhaust our own ideas first, ask for others' opinions next, and make the final decision ourselves. That way we will have considered a variety of options and possible consequences before acting in accordance with our own character and life goals.

We must also practice solo decision-making. For this, we need to identify our insecurities, fears, and causes of anger or depression; earmark something we wish to do but have a thousand reasons for not doing; then do it. Practice now is preparation for the future, boosting our self-confidence for the day that will surely come when we'll be faced with an important decision to make alone.

As you begin to flex your decision-making muscles, learn as much as you can about the situation at hand in order to make an accurate judgment, then consult your intuition to see what is right for you. While seeking counsel from your intuition, the first thought that comes to mind about the situation may well be worth examining. Why? Because you are "wired" to respond effectively to situations that influence your well-being. Even so, until you feel confident enough to rely solely on your instincts, take whatever time you need to examine their input.

Only after you have studied your first thought, and determined whether or not it is the correct course of action, is it wise to consider alternatives. As you do, continue to evaluate your options one at a time, since problems can arise from considering multiple solutions simultaneously. For one, the more possibilities there are before you, the less likely you will be to see the correct one. For another, justifying every possibility may become an excuse not to commit to a decision. When you have at last made your decision, stick to it unless you find good reason to change your mind. Learn to trust yourself.

Recently, my friend Jane purchased $1,000 of stock in a new company that was looking for investors. Soon afterward, she mentioned the opportunity to her friend Mary, who decided to purchase $1,500 worth of the stock. The next day, Mary met a man who told her he'd never heard of the company and she should not buy the stock. Mary backed out of the purchase, and two months later the company went public, increasing the value of its shares by a factor of more than 100. As a result of her insecurity, Mary allowed herself to be so easily swayed that she lost the chance to make $150,000.

If you, like Mary, renege on a decision that once felt intuitively right, find the cause for your abdication. Knowing the reason for your underlying insecurity can reinforce your efforts as you learn to trust yourself. For insights, work with exercise 8–2.

Exercise 8–2

Why Can't I Decide?

To see how much responsibility you take for your decisions, ask yourself the following questions: "Am I constantly looking to other people to tell me what to do—what job to take, where to live, or what clothes look good on me? Do I want others to validate decisions I have made?" If your answer to either one of these questions is yes, and if you want to know why you do not trust your ability to make wise choices, become more conscious of where your mind "goes" each time you have to make a decision. Finally, bring your mind back, assess your goals, then decide on a course of action.

Begin by taking small risks, then gradually work up to larger ones. Rather than be scared to make mistakes, see erring as a part of learning. Persist and you will grow a stronger self.

We spend our lives searching for security, for something that will be there when everything else is gone. But the truth is that everything on earth will at some point be destroyed, lost, stolen, or taken away. This point was driven home to me several years ago while in Bombay during a time of political violence. Soon after my arrival, I asked my cousin where I might safely travel to. "Nowhere is safe aside from sitting on the toilet," he replied. "And that, too, has its dangerous moments."

Our homes, jobs, and communities cannot be counted on to always be there. If our security lies in the love of another person, we must also acknowledge that they will not live forever. There is only one real security: knowing that we will always be there for ourselves and that we are capable of handling everything that comes our way.

How is it possible to handle *anything*? By being present in each moment—by focusing your attention on each "here and now" so your intuition can present you with thoughts and ideas. This means placing your full attention on whatever you are doing every moment of the day and night, and neither worrying about what you said or did yesterday nor dreaming about tomorrow. You will then be mentally and emotionally ready to cope with whatever comes your way and you will have the security you are looking for. In effect, if you are driving down a windy country road, the chances of reaching your destination safely will vastly improve if you look at the road rather than the clouds.

You will find it liberating to take responsibility for the decisions affecting your life. Your new self-confidence, together with your manager's and personnel's increased confidence in you, will further your business objectives. Your budding sense of security will endear you to your friends and family as well, encouraging them to see you as an equal, if not a worthy leader. Before long, *others* will be coming to *you* for decision-making advice.

Love

Real love is wanting only to give.
If you desire to possess all the wealth in the world
For no other reason than to have that much to give,
Then you know love.

If in profound meditation
Your soul, the eternal being you really are,
Touches its source, its home,
And melts in union with Divine Love—

If as you sit there
Hummingbirds land in your open palms
And chipmunks climb on your knee—
You know love.

In a state of unfathomable bliss
You return from your greatest pleasures to your worldly life
Because you know the reason you live in mortal form
Is to share what you have found.

In this sacrifice of one who knows truth
Is the pure heart of a lover
Who returns not just for the love of one out of all
But for all that have come out of One.

If you are unhappy or insecure and cannot figure out why, evaluate your life to see if it encompasses loving interactions with others. Ask yourself if people need you, or are better off because you are alive. Then check to see if you are kind to strangers or if you extend your generosity and love only to people you know. Love, compassion, and kindness, like breathing, depend on flow. If we hold our breath long enough, we will die. It is the same with love; withholding it, we cannot live a free and healthy life. Indeed, some types of depression and other health problems have been linked to a lack of love and affection.

So let your love, compassion, and kindness flow out to everyone you meet. Enroll in volunteer work—a perfect venue for giving love without having to worry about how others may interpret it. The following exercise can help you offer the gift of love in any social or professional situation.

Exercise 8–3

Letting Love Flow

To increase your capacity to let your feelings flow, try to love a person you have just met as if you had known them for twenty years. Imagine your heart melting and see what happens.

Let your love flow freely at home as well, regardless of past hurts. If you have very young children, remember they are prone to taking in information that accompanies emotions, so be careful about sending hidden negative messages along with your flow of love. Even messages that do not pertain to them will be received as if they do. For example, if you have had a hard day at work and arrive home in a bad mood, your child may internalize your comments of exasperation along with your love, quickly feeling confused, if not hurt.

Statements directed at children, even in jest, can be very harmful, since you represent someone who "knows" about the outside world. For instance, if you get cheated at work and, upon arriving home, tell your son never to go into business for himself because everyone is a liar, your son may not recognize that you are simply letting off steam. Instead, he is likely to feel the love and concern you have for him, and along with it, your anger. Subconsciously, he may learn to fear establishing a business of his own.

Both in the world and at home, refuse to let old patterns of insecurity prevent you from loving—or for that matter, from accepting love. If you want to feel loved but are reserved about extending love to others, you may be functioning through a thick filter that is inhibiting many aspects of self-expression. The more you restrict your feelings, the more impenetrable this barrier will be; conversely, the more you express your feelings, the sooner it will crumble, letting into your life a stream of true, unconditional love. The value of accepting love, compassion, and kindness from others is illustrated in the following story.

Hamid was a man of true faith. He believed that whatever happened was God's will. So no matter what Hamid was faced with, whether adversity or good fortune, he accepted his fate and said, "Eywalla"—Arabic for "As God wills it."

One day while traveling through a small village, Hamid had no money and nowhere to stay, so he asked around to see if anyone would be kind enough to put him up for the night. He was told about a wealthy man who routinely welcomed strangers. When he requested the man's address, it was given to him along with a warning: although the host was very generous to his guests, he had a strange habit of beating them up in the morning. Hamid, prepared to accept whatever God gave him, went to the wealthy man's house.

There he was greeted and invited inside. The host offered him tea and Hamid accepted, saying, "Eywalla."

Then the host asked him if he'd like to take a bath and clean up before dinner. "Eywalla" was the reply.

During dinner, the man offered Hamid his seat and the softest cushions. "Eywalla."

After a delicious meal, seconds were served. "Eywalla."

The host was so enjoying Hamid's company that he offered him a luxurious bed to sleep in. "Eywalla."

In the morning, a large breakfast was set before him, also followed by seconds. Once again Hamid responded with "Eywalla."

As Hamid was preparing to leave, the host said, "You look like you could use a bit of money to make your journey more comfortable. Please accept these few gold pieces." With great appreciation, Hamid accepted the gift, saying as before, "Eywalla."

But he was beginning to worry, for all this generosity had him convinced that he was about to get the biggest beating his host had ever delivered. Instead, the old man simply wished him a safe journey. At this point, Hamid felt compelled to speak up. "Good sir," he said, "you have been so incredibly kind and generous to me, yet I must tell you something. In the village, you have a reputation for beating your guests. Please permit me to tell the people how kind you are and that the rumors are not true."

The old man protested, saying, "No, Hamid, the stories are true. You see, you are a perfect guest; others are not so easy. When I offer tea, they say, 'No, don't trouble yourself.' When I offer extra helpings at dinner, they make such a fuss I have to ask three or four times. They go on like this throughout their stay with me, preventing me from sharing my good fortune with them. Those people are so much trouble that I always beat them up."

There is wisdom in following Hamid's example. As an aspiring practical mystic, accept what others offer you, because if you do not, you may thwart the feelings they wish to experience through giving. Even if they are giving only out of politeness, accept the offer knowing that the resulting flow of love will inspire them to be sincere. All the while, accept whatever comes your way, good or bad, with "Eywalla."

Lack of acceptance invariably leads to lack of affection. Even having an agenda for the sort of love you want is likely to derail you from the path of love—a teaching portrayed in the following story about Mulla Nasrudden, a thirteenth-century Sufi saint.

One day, recognizing that Mulla was getting old, a friend asked why he had never married. Mulla said that many years ago he had wanted to marry but didn't like any of the women in his hometown, so he set out on a journey to find the perfect wife.

He found a woman who was pretty enough but not too smart; then another who was feminine but not a good homemaker; and yet a third who had brains but not looks. Finally he found the perfect woman. She was beautiful, feminine, intelligent—everything a man could ask for.

"So, why didn't you marry her?" his friend asked.

"She was looking for the perfect man."

Chapter 9

Taking Care Of the Body

Improved physical health can accelerate our progress by increasing our available energy and our ability to focus our mind. Hence it is essential to take good care of the body.

Food

When it comes to food, the key phrase is "common sense." The best dietary guidelines, for instance, are those based on how we feel after eating. If a particular food causes us to feel bad, it would be wise to reduce or eliminate our intake of it.

Vegetarianism, although it seems to have little direct relevance to spiritual progress, can positively affect our physical health, which in turn influences our mind and spiritual growth. What is unhealthy about meat and other animal products are not the foods per se but rather the chemicals and additives they contain. Although steering clear of animal products is preferable from the standpoint of some spiritual teachings, in today's world a good option may be to eat vegetarian as often as possible and avoid being too hard on ourselves if an occasional desire arises for a hamburger or other nonvegetarian meal. In both instances, organic food is recommended.

We should also be aware that not all spiritual paths call for a vegetarian diet. For example, Sufis eat meat, although not pork. A Westerner once asked a highly evolved Sufi sheikh, "How can you eat meat? Isn't that against spiritual principles?" The sheikh replied, "When I eat the meat, I turn the cow into a Sufi." Beneath the apparent humor in his remark is the reality that Sufis, like Buddhists, Kabbalists, and followers of other traditions, approach each meal as a meditation—an occasion for honoring the "divine spark" in the food set before them. If we, too, precede our meals with a blessing that acknowledges this spark, focus entirely on the food as we eat, and conclude with a small prayer, we will both enjoy better health from our meals and further our spiritual evolution. These are the reasons for the Zen saying "When you eat, eat. When you read, read. But never eat and read."

Common sense tells us that extreme dietary limitations can have dire consequences. For one, they may lead to health problems. For another, we may find ourselves in situations where there is no choice but meat, for instance, and having developed an overly sensitive digestive system accustomed to only vegetarian foods, we may become ill after the meal. In addition, restricted eating habits may prohibit us from showing respect by eating whatever a host serves. In many cultures food is an expression of union between people at the table, hence our refusal to partake in a meal would cause a needless separation between ourselves and others. Implying that we are too pure to eat meat while everyone else is dining on it may also do us more harm than good. Unless we have a medical problem, we would do well to eat whatever others are partaking of, although in instances of squeamishness it may be best not to know what that is. In Istanbul, while slurping a soup with unidentifiable solid substances floating in it, I was glad not to know what they were.

When deciding on your diet, let the "right" foods be those that supply the nutrients your body and mind need to stay healthy. Although you need not give up animal products entirely, research vegetarian foods that provide balanced nutrition, and consider changing to a more vegetarian diet to see if it helps you feel better. Bear in mind that it can take as long as six months for your body to adjust to a new diet and for you to experience its advantages. If you feel worse during the first month or so, accept this as a normal occurrence and persevere. Also, an adequate intake of water is needed to keep the body hydrated and the limbs flexible. Tightness in the limbs, lethargy, and hyperactivity all indicate that something in your diet may need to be changed.

Fasting

Fasting helps reset the digestive system and offers a number of spiritual benefits as well. By abstaining from food, we learn to differentiate between desires of the mind and body and those of the heart and soul. We also learn to control our desires, thereby strengthening the will. It takes tremendous willpower not to eat when we are hungry and near the refrigerator. Fasting in the desert is not nearly as much of a challenge!

In addition to fine-tuning our awareness of desires and developing willpower, fasting also helps us conquer fear. Food is one of the three basic needs of the body, along with clothing and shelter, and when we go for ten days without food, we learn with certainty that we can do without it for an extended period of time with little difficulty. Once we know we can go that long with no food, the fear of not having food begins to dissipate. And when one major fear is diminished, other fears lose a bit of their stranglehold on us.

Exercise

Exercise is another important factor in maintaining physical and mental health. The mind's functioning is influenced by the condition of the brain, which operates best with a good supply of oxygen. Consequently, it is wise to do thirty minutes to one hour a day of a cardiovascular activity such as badminton, tennis, jogging, bicycling, even brisk walking—something enjoyable that gets your heart pumping and your lungs vigorously taking in oxygen and releasing carbon dioxide.

Stretching exercises are also beneficial. The flexibility stretch described below is for people of any age who wish to keep their joints flexible. For best results, practice it first thing in the morning to gently wake up your body. The vitality that results from stretching your joints upon waking can help you feel stronger and more agile as the day unfolds. If you are young and feel no need to stretch, treat this exercise as preventive medicine that can stave off joint problems later in life.

Exercise 9–1

The Flexibility Stretch

In the morning upon waking, spend ten minutes stretching each joint in your body—from those in your fingers and wrists down to those in your toes. For detailed instructions, see pages 40–41.

Joint-limbering exercises ward off stiffening by preventing the buildup of mineral deposits and ensuring that the joints continue to work smoothly and efficiently. Young children, whose bodies have not stiffened from lack of use, can easily assume positions that make their bodies appear as if they are made of rubber. Although we may not be able to recapture the flexibility we had when we were younger, we can certainly regain a good percentage of our youthful agility provided that we are willing to put in the effort. At the age of sixty, after only ten years of practice, my Tai Chi teacher in Taiwan could touch her chin to her toes while doing the splits, and she did it just as easily as you can lift this book.

Another excellent method for regaining and retaining agility is the Chinese martial art of Tai Chi, which is done in slow motion. Tai Chi concentrates on the movement of each joint and the stretching of each muscle. The results of this and other joint-limbering activities enhance meditation practices that utilize muscle control and breath to release tension.

Energy

The electrical energy that courses through the human body also extends beyond the body, forming an external electrical field known as the aura. Although we cannot ordinarily see the aura, it shows up both photographically, through such sensitive techniques as Kirlian photography, and kinesthetically, through certain movements that increase our sensitivity to the point where we can "touch" the energy. Having touched the aura, the practical mystic recognizes, with the truth of certainty, that it exists, and thus remains sensitive to its presence.

Sensitivity to the energy flowing *inside* the body is equally important. Just visualizing its flow through the marrow of our bones can often help us release physical tension and increase our energy level. When the energy flows better, so does the blood, resulting in improved eyesight, enhanced agility and reflexes, and a sharper mind.

The following pages contain a series of Tai Chi and Qi Gong exercises that can heighten your sensitivity to both external and internal energy flow. These exercises, like those of hatha yoga, are thousands of years old and have been used by great martial arts masters to perfect their being as well as their body. For best results, practice them for an hour a day—or at the very least, fifteen minutes a day—every day for the rest of your life. As you do, be sure to wear clothing that is loose enough for unrestricted breathing and movement.

In the early stages of your practice, you are likely to feel your aura, which is as much a part of your being as your arms and legs. If you wish to learn more about this electrical field, read any of the numerous books available on the subject, but believe only the information that you have proven to yourself. It may take a while to become aware of the energy that runs through your body—the life force that keeps you going from one moment to the next. Along with your experience of this energy will come enhanced sensory perceptions and increased effectiveness in all aspects of your life. The ultimate goal of external and internal energy awareness is to be able to move your body through thought alone, rather than through the energy-consuming tensing of muscles. Movement through thought conserves physical energy, reduces tension, and promotes fluid actions.

Exercise 9–2

Holding the Small Ball

Hold your hands parallel, as if clapping, keeping them one or two inches apart. Then move them slowly in opposing circles with the palms still facing each other, as if rolling a tennis ball. While maintaining this slow rotation, notice the sensations that develop in your palms. As the feeling gets stronger, gradually start to increase the distance between your hands to four or five inches. To keep your palms aligned with each other, imagine a stick extending from the center of one palm to the center of the other. Feel the energy of your aura in the center of your palms.

Exercise 9–3

Breath Raises Arms

While standing, relax your shoulders and let your arms hang loosely at your sides. Keeping your back straight, relax your breathing and all your joints as much as possible. With each inhalation, feel the breath move into your stomach as you let it expand. When you have fully inhaled, hold your breath for two to five seconds, allowing energy to build up before exhaling. Complete five more breaths in this relaxed manner. On your next inhalation, feel your shoulder blades "opening" as if your chest were expanding, and feel your arms begin to move upward on their own. As you exhale, allow your arms to gently lower.

While continuing to breathe deeply and to keep your arms relaxed, imagine your hands lifting as if someone were pulling them by the fingertips; in response, your arms will slowly rise as you inhale and drop as you exhale. Or while inhaling, mentally fill your arms with your breath, as if you were pumping in helium, and feel them float up-ward; while exhaling, release the "helium" and let them lower. Continue for about five minutes or thirty-six breaths.

*With practice, this exercise will help release tension from your neck
and shoulders. Its effectiveness will depend on the degree of mental
concentration and muscular relaxation you bring to it.*

Exercise 9–4

Holding the Big Ball

*Hold your arms outstretched at your sides, parallel with the floor
and palms facing the wall in front of you. Relax shoulders and elbows.
Prevent tension in the joints by holding your wrists an inch lower than
your shoulders, and your elbows an inch lower than your wrists. Keeping your arms straight, very slowly bring your palms together as if
you were about to clap, all the while making sure your shoulders are
relaxed.*

*As your hands approach each other, you will begin to feel something
like a huge cotton ball floating in the air between them. Once you feel
the cotton ball, stop and fluff it up very slowly. Play with it, keeping
your hands in about the same place to retain the feeling of it. Understand that what you are feeling is your aura. If you lose contact with
it, simply start over again.*

*Since the aura's energy becomes perceptible at different places for
various people, depending on their sensitivity, if you and a friend are
practicing this exercise together, do not be concerned if one of you feels
the energy when your hands are twenty-four inches apart while the
other feels it at twelve inches. Sensitivity increases with regular practice.*

*To experience a reverse polarity, bring your hands closer together;
this time, the energy of your aura will pull your hands together instead of keeping them apart as before. If you don't feel the energy at
first, keep practicing and relax your shoulders even more. Your persistence will be well rewarded.*

Exercise 9–5

Seeing Energy in the Sky

*On a clear day, stand with the sun behind you and look at the sky. Keeping your eyes unfocused, gaze at the blueness until you see sparkles, like stars flying about. Imagine this is the energy in the air referred to as **prana** in India and **chi** in China. Try to breathe in these sparkles as if you were taking in pure energy.*

The following three exercises help improve circulation and open the body's energy channels. As you practice them, you will most likely develop a greater sensitivity to the energy inside your body.

Exercise 9–6

Opening the Chest

Take a medium stance, with feet parallel and shoulder-width apart, toes pointed straight ahead, and knees slightly bent. Starting with your hands in prayer position, point your elbows out to the sides so your forearms are horizontal, and relax your shoulders. Inhale, pulling your elbows back and turning your palms to face forward. Feel your chest expand as if it were opening from the center of your rib cage. Exhale, extending your arms out to the sides, with your elbows relaxed and palms facing the side walls. Inhale, dropping your elbows to pull your arms in, with palms still facing the side walls. Move your forearms so your palms face forward. Exhale, returning your palms to prayer position. Feel your ribs squeezing the air out of your chest as you bring your hands together.

Repeat this exercise for about five minutes or thirty-six breaths, keeping shoulders relaxed, fingers extended and straight, eyes softly focused on a spot in front of you, and knees relaxed. Proceed in smooth, slow motions and at a steady pace, with no beginning or end to the movement. Your hands will feel like they are pushing through water.

Exercise 9–7

Holding the Barrel

Take a wide stance, with toes pointed straight ahead and knees un-locked. Grab the floor with your toes as if trying to pick something up with your feet. Extending your arms in front of you as though hold-ing a barrel, let the fingers of each hand point toward those of the other, about one inch apart, palms facing your navel. Focusing on the space between your fingertips, keep your chin in yet relaxed and lift your body from the crown of your head. Touch the roof of your mouth with the tip of your tongue, and relax your shoulders.

Breathe in and out through your nose with regular slow breaths, holding for one second between inhalations and exhalations, all the while expanding and contracting your belly like a bellows to gently draw in and release the air. On the inhalation, visualize the air coming in through your nostrils and moving down the center of your body to fill your belly. After you have stopped inhaling, imagine the breath continuing to fill your belly and then your arms. On the ex-halation, imagine your breath flowing out your fingertips. While con-tinuing to breathe and visualize, hold this posture for as long as possible—preferably, up to twenty minutes. As you do, relax your knees even more, keeping your buttocks tucked in; relax your hip joints, keeping your spine straight as if your body were a coat on a hanger; and relax your shoulders.

Exercise 9–8

Rotating the Shoulders

Stand with your feet parallel and shoulder-width apart, shoulders re-
laxed, arms hanging loosely at your sides, with palms facing the back
wall and fingers straight but not tense. Throughout this exercise, leave
room under each armpit as if you were holding a tennis ball there.
Concentrate on your thumbs. Inhale, turning your palms outward as
far as you can and letting your shoulders and chest open, as if your
upper torso were a book. Imagining your spine as the book's spine, try
to get the "covers" of the book to fold back by letting your shoulder
blades come as close together as possible. Turning your hands outward
as if they were being twisted by the thumbs, allow your shoulders to
rotate. Exhale, relaxing your arms and shoulders, and returning your
palms to their natural position.

Repeat this exercise for five minutes, breathing quietly. If your breath-
ing is noisy, you are probably tensing your nostrils rather than letting
your stomach expand to draw in the air and relax to release it. This
exercise is good for opening the chest and shoulders.

IV. Self-Cultivation

Chapter 10

Practices For Awakening

No words can describe an experience of enlightenment—also known as Satori in Zen and Nirvana in Buddhism. All that can be said is that an experience of enlightenment is usually a sudden, momentary, life-altering flash of startling clarity revealing a oneness with the universe and a view of our own true nature. There is also no way to summon this state of intuitive illumination. We can prepare for it, however, through the practice of being totally present in the moment—unidentified with external events, unconcerned with their outcomes, uninterested in analyzing or interpreting a thing. This is freedom. The practical mystic tills the ground for freedom through practices of awakening that train the mind to let go of thoughts, to focus, and to quiet down, aware that it can then become a receptacle for enlightenment.

This experience can come at any time. According to one Zen story, when a young disciple asked his master how he became enlightened, the master said he had meditated for forty years and then one day he was walking in the woods and fell down. When he fell, his shin hit a rock. As his shin hit the rock, he became enlightened.

For me, the experience came while I was on a bus in Taiwan after having practiced meditation and other spiritual exercises for about eight years, with no profound insights. The bus was headed for Kenting, which I verified upon boarding, and was scheduled to arrive at 3:00 in the afternoon. Well, 4:00 passed, then 5:00. By 9:00 in the evening, I saw there was no point in worrying about where we were going or when we would get there. Fully resigned to whatever would happen and free of analytical thought, I was suddenly struck full force by a clear sense of the entire universe and of myself as every part of it—every person, animal, plant, planet, and star. Overflowing with joy, I wanted to burst out laughing and exclaim, "It's all perfect!"

Because the true depth of such an experience is inexpressible, it cannot be accessed by the logical mind. Only when we let go of who we think we are and how we believe the mind functions can an experience of this nature impress itself upon us. To prepare the mind, we must train it to focus fully on the here and now, freeing it from the clutches of the lesser ego. With our mind thus focused and calm, we are able to see everything in perspective. It is toward this end that we meditate, allowing our progress to grow on its own like a newly planted tree.

A good starting point is to acknowledge just how busy the mind is. Ironically, the mind is so preoccupied it tends to overlook this reality, as the following Zen story suggests.

Two monks were in a garden watching a flag as it blew in the wind. "What's moving?" they wondered. "Is it the flag or the wind?"

The master walked by and, overhearing their conversation, said, "It is neither one. It is the mind that is moving."

The busy mind's greatest distractions are not so much what's going on outside of us as what's happening *within* us. When beset by the "noise" in our own heads, we cannot run from it, plug our ears to avoid hearing it, or turn it off. But we *can* lower the volume.

The easiest way to subdue this noise is to first know what it is and then, since we can think of only one thing at a time, to give the mind a point of focus. More often than not, the background noise is a replaying of accumulated experiences—such as a past event we feel guilty about, or the face of someone we miss. To get rid of it, we must purposefully replace it with a different thought. This is why it helps to bite your finger if your foot hurts; while focused on your finger, your mind will not register the pain in your foot. Refocusing your mind at will is a skill you can learn by working with exercise 10–1.

> Exercise 10–1
>
> ## Silencing the Background Noise
>
> *To silence the noise in your head, focus your full attention on a flower or any small object of beauty. Look at it closely, slowly taking in every detail that meets your eye.*
>
> *If an old song or some other memory comes to mind, return your concentration to your point of focus. Eventually, when you are able to focus attentively, a thought will come into your mind that may answer a question you have been grappling with for some time, or give you new information.*

If your head is frequently filled with uninvited memories, it is a good idea to develop the ability to focus on whatever is directly in front of you. Regularly making this switch will soon show you how preoccupied your consciousness is with remembering past events. Confronting the psyche's immense accumulation of past events may at first feel like fighting invisible ghosts, but the more you acknowledge their presence, the less they will taunt you and get in your way. As difficult as this problem sometimes is, it can be overcome. As J. Krishnamurti said, the answer lies in the problem itself, suggesting that you look at the problem with a completely open mind, free of preconceived ideas, as if it were someone else's dilemma being presented to you. When riddled with invasive memories, try to look at each of those thoughts as a rerun of an old TV show, then change the channel to the one you are watching today.

Another way to bring the mind into the present is to anchor it in the visceral world. The sense of touch, emphasized in exercise 10–2, offers an excellent mooring.

Exercise 10–2

Redirecting Your Attention

To stop your mind from drifting, focus on one of your hands. Concentrate on the sensations in your fingertips, the temperature of your skin and the air around it, or the texture of what you are touching. Then redirect your efforts toward your desired point of focus while simultaneously keeping your attention on your hand.

Meditation

Once freed of the mind's constant reliving of past events and analysis of present ones, we come to experience true balance and joy. That is where meditation can take us. To keep our expectations realistic, however, we first need to know where it will *not* take us. It is important to understand that although meditation can train the mind to focus exclusively on one thought, it cannot still the mind completely; in other words, meditation is not sedation. While meditating, we remain fully aware of what is going on around us yet not distracted by it.

For a basic meditation practice, try working daily with exercise 10–3. Begin by meditating quietly for ten minutes when you wake up and another ten minutes before going to sleep, gradually working up to twenty minutes each time; hour-long sessions are even better. First, choose a place that is as quiet as possible so that you will not be distracted. Then open the window to allow in plenty of fresh air; slightly cool air is best. (*Note:* If there is a great deal of noise outside, leave the window closed.) Also turn on the lights, since a brightly lit room is apt to keep you from falling asleep.

Exercise 10–3

Quiet Meditation

Sit erect, preferably in a full-lotus posture (cross-legged, with your right foot on top of your left knee and vice versa) with a pillow under your buttocks. If this is too much of a stretch, then sit in a half-lotus posture (cross-legged, with only one foot on top of the opposing knee). If you must sit in a chair, place a book under each back leg so that the seat is on a slant, then position yourself in the center of the seat to keep your spine straight and relaxed. All sitting postures help the spine relax in a naturally straight position.

With your gaze resting on a fixed spot on the floor, six to ten feet in front of you, become fully absorbed in your breath. Focus only on your breath, simply noticing the rise and fall of your chest.

If you have trouble concentrating or staying awake in quiet meditation, try meditating in a bustling cafe or crowded park. For this, follow the instructions given in exercise 10–4.

Exercise 10–4

Meditating in Public

While sitting comfortably on a bench, a chair, or the ground, focus on a fixed spot on the ground, about ten feet in front of you. Observe your breath without shifting your gaze. If people walk by or stand in your line of vision, pretend you can see right through their legs to your spot on the ground. This exercise will help develop your ability to sit in quiet meditation, and to stay focused in a busy job environment or while at home with children.

In lieu of observing your breath, you might prefer to use the Zen technique of counting from one to ten on each exhalation, simply noticing the inhalation. Or you may want to visualize your spine expanding with each inhalation and contracting with each exhalation as it pushes energy through your limbs and into the marrow of your bones.

The technique you use is less important than the consistency of your practice. Because regular meditation calms the mind, with daily practice your sleep will be more restful and your waking hours more tranquil. On days when sitting meditation is difficult, keep your practice going with active meditation, as described in the following exercise.

Exercise 10–5

Active Meditation

To train your mind to retain a point of focus through active meditation, bring your full attention to an everyday activity such as brushing your teeth or washing your face. As you do, move more slowly than usual, focusing on the bristles against your teeth or the cloth against your cheeks, tastes, temperatures, and the movement of your hand. Standing on your tiptoes while brushing your teeth or washing your face will further enhance your ability to focus.

Moving Meditations

Although daily sitting or active meditation is of great value in training the mind, on its own it is like using a small cup to empty a bucket that is filling constantly with water dripping from a faucet. Every day you will empty one cup of water from the bucket, but the drip will put half a cup back in. If you try to be conscious *every* moment of the day, however, you will empty the bucket much sooner. Each successful attempt to focus your mind—while driving, conversing, working on the computer, preparing a meal, eating, washing dishes—will remove another cup of water from the bucket. Sometimes, instead of focusing on a particular action, you might prefer to fix your attention on the sensations of a specific part of your body, such as your left foot. In either case, the more often you train your mind to focus, the more effective you will be at maintaining balance in hectic situations.

For the active Western mind, moving practices such as Kyudo (Zen archery), Tai Chi, or golf provide a welcome complement to sitting meditation. The reason is that whereas sitting meditation brings the mind to one point through no action, these practices involve the body. In Kyudo, we watch everything we are doing—picking up the arrow, placing it on the string, and drawing the bow. In Tai Chi, we watch every movement, every part of the body, and every breath. In golf, we observe our position and our swing. These practices are in many ways easier than sitting meditation since they call for momentary periods of concentration on different focal points, reining in the mind for thirty seconds, then another thirty seconds, and so on.

To benefit from moving meditations, we must be sure of our objective—which is not to become skillful at movements but rather to use them for focusing the mind. The following story illustrates the difference between developing a physical skill and developing the more profound ability to focus.

There was once a general who had spent his entire adult life fighting in wars. As he grew older, he became tired of fighting. Although a master in the arts of war, the general had but one wish: to spend the rest of his days studying Kyudo. He wanted to learn archery not to be a better fighter but rather to reflect on his inner self. Having heard of master archers in distant monasteries who had spent a lifetime perfecting their skills, he set off to find them.

After a long journey, he arrived at a monastery devoted to archery, where he requested to pass the remainder of his days. After ten years of developing his skill as an archer, however, he was approached by the master of the monastery, who said to him, "It is time for you to leave." The general was shocked and he protested, saying that his life in the outside world was over, that his only desire was to remain at the monastery and continue to meditate on the bow, the arrow, and the target. But despite his pleas to remain, he was told that to complete his training he would have to go out into the world to test his inner strength by teaching what he had learned.

Since the general could think of nowhere else to go, he returned to the village of his birth. As he walked through the surrounding forest, he noticed a bull's-eye on a tree, with an arrow in the center. The general was surprised by this, and even more startled when he observed other trees with bull's-eyes and arrows in the center. Leaving the forest, he came to farmlands, where he saw many barns and homes with bull's-eyes and arrows dead center. Agitated, he went directly to the heart of the village. There, on every wall of every building, was a bull's-eye with an arrow right in the center—each one of which stirred up such jealousy that before long he had lost all the peace he attained in his ten years of monastic life.

Indignant to find that there lived an archer more skilled than he, the general went to the village elders and demanded that the skillful archer meet him in one hour at the river by the edge of town. The general waited at the designated site, but as the hour approached no one came. Then a young girl ran up to him and asked, "Are you waiting for someone?"

"Go away," said the general, irritated.

"No, no," the girl replied. "You look like you're waiting for someone, and I was told to meet someone here."

The general looked unbelievingly at the little girl and said, "I'm waiting for the master archer who is responsible for the hundreds of perfect shots I have seen."

"Well, that's me," said the girl.

The general, feeling even more furious, looked skeptically at the child. Finally, he said, "If you are telling the truth, then explain to me how you can get so many perfect shots."

"It's easy," said the girl, brightening. "I take my arrow and I draw it back very tight in the bow. Then I point it very, very straight and let it go. Wherever it lands, I draw a bull's-eye."

Do you want to be master of a skill or master of your self? By doing Kyudo or other moving meditations to bring the mind to one-pointed concentration, you will develop the potential to perceive things you have thus far been unaware of. But to reap this reward, you must be honest about really wanting it and, unlike the general, remain true to your goal. Buddhists say, "See the Buddha as a Buddha and you will derive the benefit of being with a Buddha. See the Buddha as a man and you will derive the benefit of being with a man." In terms of your moving meditations, see your practice as a means of developing your soul and it will do so; see it as a means of developing a skill and that is all it will do.

In addition to incorporating moving meditations into your day, try to pay more attention to *every* movement you make. If you were to have sensory awareness twenty-four hours a day (yes, even while sleeping), you would be a fully conscious being always living in the present moment. To increase your awareness while performing mundane tasks, such as reaching for a glass of water or walking down the street, focus on your body movements. Try to feel your muscles as they move. Remember that your senses, like your muscles, need exercise to get stronger.

Walking Meditation

Walking meditation is helpful at any time and can have profound effects when you are depressed or angry. To meditate in this way, walk very slowly in a quiet place outdoors. If you cannot be outside, then make do with what you have, walking in circles around a room if need be. Concentrate on each step you are taking, and nothing else, not even your next step. While fully absorbed in the sensations of the foot that is moving, your mind will no longer be able to focus on what was bothering you. Then as soon as you have stopped feeding the aggravating thought, the emotion it aroused will dissolve. Do this practice for at least ten minutes at a time.

Mantras

The mind also responds well to mantras—words or phrases that inspire feelings of comfort, love, or a closeness to God. Repetition of a mantra pinpoints the wandering mind on an uplifting thought, hindering digressions into negativity or daydreaming. In the words of Tibetan lama Sogyal Rinpoche, mantra practice "protects the mind from the mind."

One day in Istanbul while on a bus with my teacher Ibrahim, I noticed that he was constantly repeating "Allah, Allah, Allah." As soon as I spoke, he would stop and converse with me; when we finished, he would immediately return to his mantra. Even at age seventy he was keeping his mind focused every minute so it would not drift off to negative thoughts.

Because mantra practice inspires feelings, it is also able to help us bypass the mind and link us directly with our essence. Despite all the practices we may undertake and the multitude of self-improvement tips we may follow, if there is no emotion in our efforts, the mind is apt to remain in charge. When focused on a mantra, however, this controlling part of us can give way to the voice of intuition. Repeating a mantra of your own, as described in the following exercise, is an ideal occupation for your mind any time you are not engaged in a conversation or in a task that requires your full attention.

Exercise 10–6

Create Your Own Mantra

*To create your own mantra, think of a word or short phrase that has special meaning to you. A possibility might be **There is God,** or **I am at peace,** or even **God, God, God,** or **Peace, Peace, Peace.** Once you have found your mantra, repeat it continually while driving, walking, eating, going to sleep, and upon waking. With great emotion, say your mantra either out loud or in an audible whisper, trying it in different tones to see which one brings the best results. You may feel various parts of your body reverberating in response to the diverse tones.*

When you are sufficiently devoted to this practice and deeply affected by it, the mantra will be your first thought upon waking and will pop into your mind to calm you down in difficult situations throughout the day. At this point you are also likely to notice that the inspiring thought introduced by your mantra is regularly replacing a troubling one, decreasing the occurrence of insomnia, moodiness, and depression. For best results, persistence is imperative.

For even better results, Sufis add a second mantra. Why? Because the brain and mind function independently. While the brain is focusing attention outwardly, the mind can easily drift to other thoughts without our knowing it. Hence for full attention training, we must work on both levels simultaneously. To begin this practice, choose a second mantra, then say it out loud while repeating the original mantra silently in your mind. Ideally, both mantras should be the same length so that you can start and end them together.

To go further with this practice, add a visualization by picturing a person you emulate. For example, while repeating the mantra *Truth, Truth, Truth,* envision the person you believe is most representative of truth. In Sufism, ethereal Khidr guides spiritual seekers; hence you may want to think "Khidr" and say *Truth* out loud while picturing Khidr in your mind. Or you might prefer to picture a historical person such as the Buddha, Gandhi, or Abraham Lincoln. The important point is to work simultaneously with all three aspects— thought, verbalization, and visualization. With practice, this technique can go a long way toward helping you sustain a meditative state.

Breathing

Another method for improving your concentration is to observe your breathing intermittently throughout the day. While waiting to order in a restaurant or while standing in line at the post office, try following your breath, described in exercise 10-7. This breathing practice can take place even while other people are conversing with you.

Revealing the fact that you are doing a meditation is not recommended, since it may prompt negative remarks from others, which could be distracting. It may also encourage your lesser ego to turn your practice into a demonstration of how good you are to be meditating. To benefit from your efforts, simply follow your breath and keep all explanations to yourself.

Exercise 10–7

Following Your Breath

To improve your concentration, breathe in slowly and evenly. With chest, neck, and shoulders relaxed, notice your breath as it enters your nostrils and mentally direct it down the center of your torso and into your abdomen. All the while, let your mind follow its movement as if drawing a line with a pen. While exhaling, visualize your breath flowing out the front of your abdomen.

Identity Awareness

To uncover the true nature of your mind, let it become fully absorbed in identifying exactly who is behind the actions you are performing. Silently ask yourself: "Who am I? Who is doing _____ (whatever it is you are doing at the moment)? Who is making my brain tell my body how to move?" This examination, too, can be conducted in the presence of other people, since no one will notice what you are doing. Unlike self-observation, it will keep your mind occupied with a question rather than objectively observing your actions.

An alternative approach is to contemplate a Zen koan. A koan is a riddle with no possible answer, similar to "What is the sound of one hand clapping?" It encourages you to meditate on the unanswerable question until the logical mind gives up and shuts down for a moment, allowing you a direct glimpse at reality. To enhance your identity awareness, a good question to focus on is "Who was I before I was born, and who will I be after I die?"

If you practice paying attention through moving meditations, breathing, and questioning as often as possible from the time you wake up until you fall asleep, your sitting meditation will be far more effective. These practices will also help you progress if for any reason you cannot do sitting meditation. Even a twenty-minute practice session will be beneficial.

Exercises for Awakening

The following exercises, except where noted, can be practiced every day as further aids to awakening. Choose one or however many you would like to work with, and stay with the routine for at least two months before adding or eliminating exercises. To develop willpower, force yourself to practice daily no matter what.

❖ Do automatic writing for ten to thirty minutes at least twice a week.

❖ Do physical exercises for fifteen to thirty minutes each morning, in addition to stretching your fingers, wrists, feet, neck, and eye muscles.

❖ Sit in quiet meditation for at least twenty minutes before going to sleep and again upon waking. As you do, observe your breath, repeat your mantra, or simply sit.

❖ Regularly notice the physical sensations in your body: tensions, feelings, temperatures, and so forth.

❖ Make a checklist of your chosen exercises to show yourself how serious you are about awakening. Use it to record your practice sessions and to evaluate daily how well you are progressing. If you prove to be lazy, you may not be as serious as you thought, which might motivate you to work harder.

❖ Be honest with yourself. Devote one day a week to truthfulness—neither lying nor exaggerating. Spend first one hour, then half the day, then the entire day saying and doing nothing you would have to apologize for. This includes refusing to agree to anything you do not intend to participate in, such as a lunch date or a phone conversation.

❖ Walk down the main street of town looking straight ahead; do not turn your head to look at stores, pedestrians, or traffic, except while crossing the street. Simply focus on your breathing or your mantra, or on feeling the ground beneath your feet.

❖ Sit in a busy cafe or restaurant, and read. Concentrate on your reading material without getting distracted.

❖ Observe your thoughts and feelings while conversing with others. Smile at everyone you interact with, including waiters and waitresses, giving *sincere* attention to their feelings. When alone, be attentive to all your movements and do not let yourself be clumsy.

❖ Determine the motivation for your actions and desires. Look for subtle intentions beneath the apparent ones.

❖ List everything you dislike or hate, questioning the reasons for each of these feelings. You may find that the root cause of a troubling situation has nothing to do with present circumstances, but is instead related to a past event, a previous relationship, or childhood programming. Clearing the antipathy will free you up to enjoy plunging into activities you have been avoiding.

❖ Judge everything according to your personal experience. Never take another person's opinion as absolute truth; listen and assume that it may be true if the source is reliable, but verify it for yourself. Be especially cautious about accepting what one person tells you that another has said, or thirdhand information.

❖ Four times a day, take regularly scheduled three- to five-minute breaks to work with self-observation or a meditative practice. Select exercises that you can do around other people so you will have no reason to skip a practice. To strengthen self-discipline, do the same exercise at the same time each day. If you miss one session, make it up as soon afterward as you can. Your practice can be as simple as counting 30 breaths or doing 100 mantra repetitions, counting them on a small string of prayer beads in your pocket.

❖ While performing a familiar task such as washing dishes, housecleaning, or walking, count from 1 to 100 and back again, then count every second number and back, then every third number and back. Counting will keep your mind awake and focused, and unlikely to drift off in a daydream.

❖ Eat a meal in silence, looking only at your food and visualizing where it came from. Think of the fish swimming in the ocean, the chicken running around the farm, the broccoli growing in the field, the golden wheat swaying in the wind. Appreciate that everything on your plate existed so that you could live.

❖ Eat a meal blindfolded, experiencing what it might be like not to have the use of your eyes. Or tie one hand behind your back and feel what life might be like without the use of your arm. This exercise can help you develop compassion for others and gratitude for your capacities.

❖ Eat a meal in slow motion. Moving slowly and deliberately, watch each of your gestures, absorbed in them as if there were nothing else in the world.

❖ While doing chores such as washing dishes or laundry, each time you touch an item think of the person who used it. Remind yourself of how much you love that person, and feel the connection you have with them.

❖ Regardless of what you are looking at or listening to, keep your mind in your heart. Do this by imagining the tickle of a little fly crawling around on the center of your chest. Western science does not know where the mind is; Eastern teachings, however, place it in the heart area. Therefore, keeping the mind in the heart means keeping your attention focused on the center of your chest. Maintaining this focus while zeroing in on an immediate goal, as in archery practice or any slow-moving activity, can enormously increase your rate of accuracy. Doing it while looking at other people can help you feel the unity in all beings—a profound experience.

Chapter 11

Discovering Your Life's Direction

I once told the head monk of a Zen monastery in Japan that I wanted more than anything to retire from the world and become a hermit monk. At the same time, I seemed to have abilities pointing me in another direction: people I knew, as well as strangers, would often tell me their business problems, and for some reason I was able to offer solutions, renewing their sense of hope. When I told this to the monk and explained that I was a very successful businessman, he replied that some individuals are meant to be monks whereas others are meant to be businesspeople, garbage collectors, artists, or any number of other occupations. He said we must each do what we are good at, meditate daily, and every day make someone smile.

Taking his words to heart, I began to view life as a circle encompassing certain fields of possibility. I envisioned that the portion we see at any given moment, although only a piece of the circle, contains a wide selection of options. As we move undistractedly in one direction, smaller circles keep appearing, guiding us along a path that more clearly defines our purpose. Eventually we can look back and notice all the previous circles superimposed one on top of the other in the form of a target, and there we are at the bull's-eye.

Like Kyudo, this method of focusing our perception amid the tug of numerous possibilities has us hitting the bull's-eye of our destiny. In mastering this technique, we can make our life flow like an arrow directly to the point of our reason for being. Having struck the bull's-eye, we simply retrieve the arrow and proceed with another shot, which in turn brings us closer to the next target. Endlessly proceeding, we are forever evolving.

Finding Your True Purpose in Life

The search for our true purpose in life is what makes the difference between mere existence and an extraordinary unfolding. There are many things to do in the world, yet for some reason we seem to think that either all the "slots" have been filled or that someone else is already doing what we would enjoy—and doing it far better than we ever would. However, with a strong mind and an adventurous spirit, anything becomes possible.

While trying to discover your true purpose, do not be concerned with what anyone else says about you or your desires. If you are already trying to do something other than what you enjoy, ask yourself why. Then redirect your course—not by fixing what was broken in the past, but by bringing the future into the present. In other words, develop a clear picture of what you want to be, then start living as if it has already come to pass. Waiting for something to happen in the future is not beneficial. For one thing, those who patiently sit and wait often get someone else's leftovers. For another, the vessel must be formed before the wine can be poured in. And you form the vessel by living the way you want to live, for only then can opportunities come your way. So rather than wait for the perfect destiny to be delivered to your door, put forth the effort to get what you want. Talk to people in your community, look around to see what is needed, read the Yellow Pages. You may find just the field for you, or perhaps be inspired to start a new venture of your own. Then plunge in. If you discover that you want to be a great artist, for instance, paint as well as you can today and you'll be a better artist tomorrow.

The two major obstacles to discovering our true purpose in life are lack of self-confidence and the negative opinions of others. On the one hand, we may have found exactly what we would like to do, but not paid much attention for fear that we were not good enough to succeed at it. On the other hand, we may have been discouraged upon mentioning a particular calling to friends or family members. For instance, if your father, although uninformed about opportunities in your chosen field, said it would never generate enough income, his statement may have stopped you in your tracks. In both instances, the way to climb out of the void is by pursuing your passion. Even if you do not make it your profession, doing what you love as a hobby can change your life.

Begin by rearranging your priorities so that you can do what you love rather than what is expected of you or what is currently in vogue. Setting new priorities will most likely mean eliminating one activity or another to make time to follow your passion. After all, do you know anyone who has free time to work on a new activity on a regular basis? If you wait for free time to appear in your life, you may end up waiting forever.

The following question-and-answer exercise can help you discover your true path. If possible, have someone else ask you the questions, then reply as honestly as possible—or better yet, tape record your answers and transcribe them later. The important points are to contemplate each question thoroughly before responding and to write or say whatever comes to mind, without editing your answers or checking them for logic or feasibility.

Exercise 11–1

What Is My Path?

Approach this exercise as if you were assembling a two-piece jigsaw puzzle. To create the first piece of the puzzle, answer these questions: What activities do you enjoy? What are your talents, skills, and personality traits? List every positive thing about you, such as playing piano, painting, problem solving, computer work, or ability to organize. Then explain why you like each of these pursuits.

To come up with the second piece of the puzzle, reply to these questions: What did you most enjoy or fantasize about as a child? What special game did you love to play with friends or on your own? What do your parents and siblings remember about your childhood interests and passions?

*Now creatively link your childhood activities to a potential occupa-
tion, either one that exists or one you could invent. For example if, as a
child, you dreamed of flying, then consider becoming a pilot or doing
other aviation-related work, or exploring the world of model airplanes.
If you loved making up games or playing with toys, think of possible
inventions for kids or an aspect of the toy business you might enjoy.
Any time you note hesitation or find yourself ruling out possibilities,
search for the root cause of your reaction. As you persist in asking why
you have a problem with a particular profession, you may come up
with feelings of self-doubt, insecurity, or discouragement. Regard your
root causes of hesitation as keys to freeing yourself from long-perceived
limitations.*

When he was very young, a boy named Joseph Caventou asked
his mother, "Why are plants green?" His mother replied that she
didn't know and he ought to go find out for himself. Undaunted, and
with much help from others, he went on decades later to discover
chlorophyll. So it is that childhood questions and dreams can lead to
purposeful and important work, provided that wonder and desire are
not squelched in the interim. It is for this reason that childhood
interests form an integral piece of the jigsaw puzzle that can help us
find our true path.

As you will see, piecing together your purpose in life is more challenging than assembling a jigsaw puzzle, since there is no way to
know in advance what the finished picture will look like. Moreover,
the pieces of present and past pleasures may not appear the least bit
related to each other. All you can do is remain open to the possibility
of links between them. In fitting the pieces together you will get sections; fitting the sections together will give you the whole picture.
For now, be content with fitting the pieces together.

I recently practiced exercise 11–1 with a young woman who saw
her life as a struggle and her destiny as an endless chase in pursuit of
one menial job after another to earn money. However, while

answering the questions, she discovered that she was interested in drawing and photographing people, especially faces. She also liked observing people from a distance, looking at their expressions, and wondering what thoughts and experiences had brought such character to their faces. She also liked fashion, because it showed people's moods and tastes.

At first glance, we thought she could be an artist, a photographer, or a fashion coordinator or designer. But looking more closely at her *reasons* for enjoying these pursuits, I saw they were all connected to a fascination with people's personalities. I therefore suggested she explore psychology, and she immediately lit up. She then remembered that she had taken a psychology course some years before, had found it extremely interesting, and had scored high marks with little studying. Interlocking her past with her present, she was able to see that her true purpose in life was indeed to work in the field of psychology.

But after her initial elation over this discovery, she became plagued by doubts, concerned about the competition among psychologists. I then suggested that while pursuing psychology in school, she might look for what was *not* being taught and, like Sigmund Freud, Carl Jung, and other pioneers of the psyche, perhaps develop a new branch in the field, offering her own unique contribution. Sufis say that no one knows another person's destiny—a teaching that was paramount in my mind when I suggested branching off. Not knowing if this young woman was meant to change the world, or even her little part of it, I told myself that anything was possible. Sure enough, within a month she was working toward a degree in a field that filled her with joy and excitement.

Movement brings opportunity. So once you, too, have interlocking pieces in the jigsaw puzzle of your true purpose, reorient yourself and start moving. Enroll in a course of study, apply for a position that promises on-the-job training, or apprentice with an inspiring mentor. If you feel called to be an innovator, learn the basics and then follow your heart.

Changing Your Goals

The search for your true purpose requires a readiness to change. To begin with, a goal that *appears* to be what you want may have been dictated by your lesser ego out of a desire to control you. To find out for sure, examine each idea that arises to see if it springs from your essence, your childhood programming, or one of your little I's. You will know a goal that is aligned with your true purpose by the excitement it generates in you. Once you have found this goal, rearrange your priorities and begin to move toward it.

Another occasion for changing goals may arise while pursuing one idea and being tempted to jump off it to another one. In this instance, it is best to give the first idea a fair trial period, since it may turn out to be an invaluable stepping stone to your true goal. Therefore, although it is important to prepare for change, consider staying with an endeavor that once felt right, all the while checking to see if it might propel you toward a larger goal. If you feel content and at peace, know that you are most likely on the right path, even if you are uncertain about where it is taking you. If your initial enthusiasm has mellowed and your pursuit is bringing you happiness but not fame, remember that even though you may not be altering the planet you are still affecting *someone.* Remember, too, that dedication to a goal that turns out to be a stepping stone has payoffs of its own: it can lead to the discovery of your ultimate goal or to the acquisition of knowledge that will help you accomplish it.

When it does come time to take the leap to a new path, understand that changing a life goal can be intimidating, especially if you lack self-confidence. This hurdle can be cleared through practice in surmounting other insecurities. For example, if you are scared of knives, as I once was, learn to sharpen them and use them often, starting with a small pocketknife and working up to a carving knife, or perhaps a machete. Once you are comfortable with knives, you will have increased confidence to tackle the shift to your new path. By then you will also know that what was frightening was not knives per se, since on their own they cannot cause injury, but rather your lack of self-awareness. "What if I am not careful?" you may have wondered, or "What if I fall into a conscious sleep while handling a knife?" The root cause of many terrors and insecurities is fear of the lack of control we experience in our sleeping state—in effect, fear of *ourselves*.

Because we are forever learning and evolving, we need to observe ourselves and reassess our goals at each stage of the journey, if not on a daily basis. By examining ourselves regularly, noticing who we are becoming and how we are behaving, we can nip negative personality traits in the bud and maintain a clear picture of what we wish to achieve.

Recognizing Your Destiny

A common concern among people searching for their life's direction is the question of how much control we really have over the course of our lives. In India we would be told, "You can do what you want, but the outcome will still be the same." In the long run this may be true, but how we get there does seem to entail freedom of choice. I like to think of destiny as the palm of a hand, with each finger offering a path of its own as well as a unique set of other possible destinies. Some of these paths lead to happiness, whereas others lead to difficulties—both of which are part of the palm of destiny. In a state of equanimity, we are able to look deep within ourselves and discover the best path to take. At the very least, equanimity can prevent us from running in circles, refusing to decide which path to take.

In practical terms, destiny can be defined as the most peaceful path in life—one in which pain and suffering are only momentary experiences. A life filled with troubles results more often than not from a *failure* to follow the path of destiny. One way to tell whether or not you are following the path to your destiny is to evaluate how you feel after making a decision: Are you at peace or in turmoil? If you feel peaceful, you are probably on your path. If you are in turmoil, use the self-observation exercises in chapter 2 to determine whether the torn feelings are from your soul or from one of your fearful I's.

Some years ago my destiny was to return to the Sufis in Turkey. I had been traveling through Europe when I suddenly began to feel an increasing undercurrent of unrest, which lasted for days until I booked a flight to Istanbul, where it instantly dissolved. Frequently, we cannot sense that we are going against our destiny until the discomfort is extreme. Yet prolonged turmoil is not the only indicator of wrong direction; intuition gives us this information as well, and even more quickly, provided that we pay attention to it. And the sooner we hear the call of destiny, the sooner our life will run more smoothly. Indeed, every aspect of life brightens when we are listening to the music of our intuition rather than the background noise of interfering thoughts. Even if it takes years to learn to hear our intuition, there is great consolation: the remaining years will bring immense pleasure to compensate for our efforts.

Following our life's destiny happens one step at a time as we tread the path of each little destiny. If while engaged in a conversation we are preoccupied with thoughts about what we will say next, we will not be able to hear what is being said. It is the same with following our destiny; if we are busy plotting our next move, we will not be able to hear the voice of intuition. To hear the call of destiny, we must be quiet enough for clear thoughts to enter our mind.

We are like sailors on the ocean, and destiny is the wind. If we are asleep, we cannot control our boat; to make matters worse, the sails are serving as bedcovers. However, if we awaken we can raise the sails, feel the wind blowing, and steer the boat to its destination. Our ability to steer it is directly related to our level of wakefulness.

Progressing with Teachers

Just as food is useless if the mouth is closed, so is guidance from a teacher useless if the mind or heart is shut down. My Sufi teacher, Ibrahim, says that the heart is the veil to the soul, which is where we find our true self and our destiny. Consequently, it is important to cleanse the heart—a process that happens naturally when we are being honest. Accepting the truth about ourselves, even if it seems bad, is cleansing.

All Eastern mystical teachings stress the importance of a teacher for those on the path to personal growth. A teacher provides many benefits—among them, the experience of unconditional love. As students, we see our teacher's skills as far superior to ours and marvel at how he patiently gives of his time and effort to help us when he could be engaging in endeavors more suited to his own level of development. This patient giving can inspire in us such a deep appreciation and admiration for our teacher that unconditional love wells up in our hearts. Because we are in the presence of someone expressing this love, we come to understand our own feelings more clearly and to distinguish between real love and what we thought was love—namely, infatuation activated by the lesser ego or the body to fulfill its needs. The love without demands that a teacher awakens is not often found in family or society.

An inspiring teacher need not be a spiritual instructor; he could be a teacher of any subject. The important point is to associate with a person who is endowed with qualities of selfless giving, so that you will have a living example to ignite your heart-cleansing honesty and unconditional love.

For further progress, practice exercises for awakening and read ancient teachings that transmit knowledge through analogies and parables. As you do, be sure to contemplate the hidden wisdom and find ways to make practical use of it rather than simply filing it away in your mind. Although it is possible to learn from disciplined practices or books, in terms of spiritual growth there is no replacement for a human teacher.

The teacher you choose to associate with should have the best interests of his students at heart. One way to determine this is to see if he relies on his students for financial support or if he lives for the benefit of his students, placing no demands or expectations on them. The sheikhs of the Sufis I was with in Istanbul always had their own jobs or businesses; in fact, they often give money and other forms of support to their disciples!

Safer Dal Efendi, my Sufi sheikh, owned a candy store and my Tai Chi master, Bing Lee, is a salesman for a printing company. They both appear quite ordinary yet possess extraordinary abilities. Great humility is always a trait of a true master, so you never know who you are dealing with. Both these men, even after forty years at their practice, still patiently welcomed the opportunity to teach beginners.

Since false teachers are as prevalent now as ever before, an evaluation of this sort is essential. *A word of caution:* It is impossible to access the soul by simply imitating a teacher, as the following story illustrates.

A great Sufi master, the most evolved and admired being of his time, who had thousands of devoted disciples, decided to take a wife. He chose the nastiest, rudest, most ignorant woman he could find. Every day, she would curse and ridicule him in public, and in private treat him in a manner that would make any man's life a complete hell. Yet through it all, the master smiled and complied. Never did he argue or defend himself.

One day, a disciple asked why he had taken such a woman as his wife. Surely, a master as great as he must have known what this woman would bring to him, the young man thought to himself. The master replied, "Since so many of you regard me with great esteem, I am in danger of being misled by my ego and losing my way. I have taken such a wife to balance the praise I receive from other people I am with every day. That way I will not become arrogant and think myself greater than God."

The disciple, accepting this path as his own, found himself a similar wife. As a result, he soon became so miserable that he began to contemplate suicide. He then told the master what he had done and asked for advice. The master explained, "You have taken someone else's medicine. The illness of the ego that I faced was not endangering you, yet you took my medicine. And so what heals me has hurt you."

We cannot progress by imitating others. Indeed, each one of us must endure the pains of our own path before we can develop wisdom. Knowing this, we may be assured that the mastery available through a guide who shows the way far surpasses anything we can gain on our own.

Assessing Personal Growth

The more growth we achieve the freer we will be from the dictates of the lesser ego. This equation holds true on the material plane of physical and personality needs, as well as on other levels of being. In terms of spiritual growth, the practices of awakening promise great success because they redirect energy once wasted on fears and worries into energy we can use to improve our business skills and quality of family life. However, even when we have worked hard at self-improvement, we may not be progressing as much as our lesser ego would like us to think we are, as is illustrated by the following humorous story.

Two successful lawyers were praying together in a temple. Engaged in a humility practice, they were hitting themselves and saying repeatedly, "I'm nothing, I'm nothing." When the janitor sat next to them and joined in this practice, one lawyer said to the other, "Look who thinks he's nothing."

Taking credit for charitable acts we have performed indicates that we have not yet begun to awaken, since our actions were governed by a need of the lesser ego for recognition. If they happen to work out well, the results should be attributed to good fortune rather than our own doing. To wake up, we need to practice humility, as expressed in the axiom "If we do a good deed and no one knows who did it, we did a great thing. If we do a good deed and one person knows, we did a good thing. If we do a good deed and everyone knows, we did nothing." Once awakened, we will realize that our entire existence is between our self and our god, and has nothing to do with what anyone else says or thinks about us. This state, described earlier as the Sufi definition of freedom, is what the practical mystic is attempting to achieve in seeking unity with God and freedom from the lesser ego—in short, equanimity.

Both observing how the lesser ego wants to take credit for our actions and expressing true humility are important for personal development. Expressing true humility implies *not* taking credit for our actions. This does not mean that upon receiving a compliment we should put ourselves down and say, "Oh, it was nothing," or "I am not really any good"—signs of a lesser ego fishing for praise. It is simply to suggest that we should not let the compliment go to our head. This is at the heart of the Buddhist message carved in stone at Thailand's Wat Pra Suthep temple, which reads: "As a rock is unmoved by wind or rain, so a wise man is unmoved by praise or blame." Nor should we point out our deeds if they have gone unnoticed. Always, we must remember that we are not the most important beings in the world. What needs to get done will get done—if not by us, then by someone else.

As you continue to uncover the manipulative behavior of the lesser ego, you will notice yourself engaging in a variety of negative feeling states and actions—everything from fear of criticism to pride to lying. The lies, directed most often at yourself, will have you convinced that acts you have performed were for the sake of others when in reality your lesser ego was showing off to win praise. A sign of personal growth emerges when you are unaware of having performed a task for others until someone happens to mention it.

The importance of humility was also understood by the powerful and wise Alexander the Great, who had conquered most of the known world by the age of thirty-two. When he knew he was dying, he offered half his kingdom to anyone who could save him, but the doctors all replied that it was not possible, for he was going to die. So he left instructions that when the funeral procession went to the burial grounds, his hands were to be left hanging out of the coffin. And after he was buried, the stone placed on his grave was to read: "Here lies Alexander the Great, world conqueror—born with nothing, died with nothing."

Knowing the truth makes us tranquil, whereas living with illusion creates turmoil. An agitated mind filled with random thoughts can neither see truth nor dictate appropriate actions. Only through meditation, Tai Chi, or other practices used to calm body and mind are we able to observe our intentions while remaining unattached to results.

Learning through Failure

In our work toward self-improvement, we must not let errors discourage us. If ever we forget that it is normal to make mistakes, and begin to punish or condemn ourselves, then our lesser ego will have won. As in Tai Chi, where we use the opponent's energy to our own advantage, we can use the lesser ego's attempts to obstruct our progress as a launchpad to success. We take a great leap forward the moment we acknowledge how creative the lesser ego is in its endeavors to trick us, and as a result refuse to follow its directives.

We are free to do as we will. We are also at liberty to decide what is valuable and true, and what is irrelevant. We can take people's negative judgments personally and feel like a failure, or we can dismiss their comments entirely. If we see ourselves as a failure, we will be unable to gain significant ground on the path to awakening and achieving our goals. The best preventative is to understand that the perception of failure is a result of either early programming or the illusion of permanence.

The illusion of permanence is rooted in the belief that thoughts and material objects alike are permanent and therefore possess great power. The illusion, according to Buddhist thought, is that *anything* is permanent. When we realize that all thoughts and objects are instead temporary, we can free ourselves from fear of failure and continue our progress. One way to recognize the transitory nature of a thought is by recalling, from exercise 1–4, that we do not know ourselves as well as we thought we did. This means that any pain, difficulty, or lack of fulfillment will someday end, and that every possession will slip away. In all respects, life as we know it is best lived in keeping with the saying "This, too, shall pass."

When we no longer believe in illusions, all that is left is truth. Hence the way to see truth is by eliminating illusions. Like walking around the world, eliminating illusions is very simple, but it takes a long time to cover that much territory. To shorten the journey, we can stop allowing fear of failure—or fear of success, for that matter—to get in our way. Rudyard Kipling's beautiful poem "If" says it best, for there he reminds us that "If you can keep your head

when all about you / Are losing theirs and blaming it on you. . . .
Yours is the Earth and everything that's in it."

Staying on the Path

Sufi teachings tell us that if we stray from the path of spiritual
seeking, or fail to follow it when the time is right, we will lose our
money, our family, and then our health. These losses are gifts
bestowed by God to encourage us to seek truth. Regrettably, it is
often in suffering that we seek the path to our essence, where we
find deep peace and contentment. Rarely will we get out of a warm
comfy bed to walk barefoot in a cold room unless someone pulls the
covers off of us.

Sometimes we try to follow a path and then stray from it for the
sake of an easier life. The lesser ego—striving to keep us ignorant of
our destiny—tricks us into thinking that we have not strayed but are
simply finding a better way. Other times, considering ourselves
stronger than we really are, we believe we can follow our true path
and still stay in control of the lesser ego, only to find that such a feat
is impossible. In fact, the further we progress, the more difficult it
can be to watch the ego setting booby traps each step of the way. In
reality, we cannot simply walk away from a path of knowledge and
return to a life of ignorance. If we wish to be a seeker of truth, we
cannot take even one step backward; the person we were must continually give in to the one we truly are.

As we become more expressive of our true self, we place less
emphasis on wanting people to like us. We begin to say what we see
as the truth—behavior old friends and family members may not
appreciate. As Tibetans say: "Dog doesn't like being beaten with a
stick; human doesn't like to hear the truth." If we are serious about
our progress, we will begin to see, speak, and live the truth of every
situation, which will naturally upset people who would much rather
live in their illusions. To preserve the status quo and persuade us to
return to how we were, they may do everything in their power to
try to convince us that what we are doing is bad and that we have
become a terrible person. The fact is that people fear truth seekers,

because they demonstrate the possibility of change. And if one person begins to change for the better, then others will see that they also can improve. Since the effort required to change is far too great for most people, instead of accepting that they are not what they could be, they would rather eliminate the cause of their realization—which is why seekers in the process of awakening often come under attack.

To strengthen your resolve to stay on the path of self-improvement, consider taking certain days of the year, or the first day of each month, on retreat to look back and see the progress you have made. Also record new developments in your journal of changes—preferably, as you see them happening rather than later when they may be a foggy memory. For example, if one day you are interacting with someone who consistently arouses uncontrollable anger in you, and you do not fall into the same old pattern, make a note of this. Then when someone else later tells you that what you are doing is not good, or that you are becoming a nasty person, read your journal to verify that, to the contrary, you are experiencing visible signs of progress. Remind yourself that some people simply fear change and are ill-equipped to handle the unknown. Resolve not to lose the self-confidence and progress you have gained.

Being of Service

If you are unable to find your purpose in life, try serving humanity every chance you get. Volunteer your time as a mentor, or a Big Brother or Sister; offer to bullyproof your local elementary school; join a volunteer fire department or neighborhood association; shovel snow for an elder; serve tea. To serve is to be useful, and being useful can instill in you a sense of purpose. As that feeling grows, your true purpose may emerge. Do not speak of your acts or expect credit for them; just do as much as you can, knowing that your actions are helping to build a better world. In time, life will return a service to you. This is the karma yoga path of self-refinement, doing for others without feeding the ego with rewards.

If you perform charitable deeds for the good of humankind,

remember that this alone will not make you a great person. Conversely, you are not a bad person for not serving others. It is said that our place in heaven is determined by what we *intended* to do, not necessarily by what we did. For instance, a person whose thoughts and emotions veer toward killing, cheating, or stealing, even if they never perform these acts, may attract similar deeds, or at least encounter hard times in the future. As for the world we are in now, it will be a better place if we all try to do the best we can.

What is life like for a person who is not in touch with his purpose for being? A perceived lack of purpose leads to a lack of self-respect. A person who feels he has no reason for being—nobody he can help, or no work that seems useful—may have a hard time justifying his existence. To avoid being overwhelmed by his lack of self-worth, he may choose to remain asleep.

Few of us are exempt from this problem. Children lose their self-respect when they are put down in school because their grades are not good enough, or when their parents believe they should be "seen, not heard." A competitive atmosphere, too, although stimulating to some, can eradicate self-respect in others. A wise person will treat others with respect and appreciation simply for being, which alone can help them feel wanted, needed, and purposeful. The reason we succumb so easily to feelings of worthlessness is that our soul growth has been hampered by our deluding lesser ego. We live with such illusions that anything we have decided not to do because we believe we have already mastered it is probably something we *must* do. For example, if we proclaim with great conviction that we do not talk too much, we probably do. Someone I knew once said in all seriousness, "I used to be conceited, but I'm over that. Now I'm perfect."

We all have a purpose in life, and to find it we must have contact with our essence, which means we must break through the fears and negativity generated by the lesser ego. Selfless service tames the lesser ego, at once freeing us from its shackles, nourishing our self-esteem, and setting us on the path to discovering our life's purpose.

Are you ready to take this journey? If so, remove illnesses of the soul—arrogance, envy, and anger, as well as gossip, greed, and fear—and unburden your essence. Eliminate illnesses of the heart, such as negative thoughts and feelings, consciously filling the void with positive thoughts and feelings. The resulting clear spirit will bring you to the brink of health, happiness, and truth. While visiting friends in India, I was told, "If there is love in the heart, there is plenty of room in even the smallest of places. If there is no love in the heart, then there is no space for one ant in the whole world."

Preparing for Death

Everyone and everything that exists will someday die. Whatever we have accomplished or built or acquired will be irrelevant to us in a hundred years. Even planets and stars have a fixed life span. Recognizing that all material forms of life meet the same end, we feel inspired to search for a root cause of these creations and a way to take proper leave of the body when the time comes.

Just as the moon reflects the sun's light, our world reflects the energy of its creator. Similarly, the body we inhabit reflects the energy of its creator—a source that remains hidden from view by a living body. Looking for the source, rather than being blinded by the reflection or expression of it, can help us expand our vision beyond the material world to the cause of existence.

Searching for the source requires confronting the unfathomable and pondering age-old questions: If there is no God, and this world and all its beings are here by chance, what is the point of human existence? If there is a God, why are things so confusing and why is he so elusive? If God is a hidden treasure and wants to be known, as Sufis say, why does he hide from that which he created to know him? Is God a word used to convey a concept or is God a being?

To approach an understanding of God, consider the transition between life and death. Think about what constitutes the difference between a living person and a dead one. At a certain point, something leaves the body and turns it from a human being into a corpse. That which gives the body life and then eventually leaves is what you really are—and is permanent. The belief that your *body* is you is an illusion. In this sense, accepting death as inevitable is freeing, rather than morbid. When you truly know that your life continues past the death of the body, you will no longer be so attached to this life and so identified with fears. So, while living this life, feel compassion for all beings, yet realize that death is the normal progression of life and that this life is only a blink in the eye of the universe. In short, do not get stuck believing that what happens here on earth is permanent. To expand your vision, work with exercise 11–2.

Exercise 11–2

Beyond-the-Body Meditation

Imagine you are at your own funeral. As you watch your body lying in wait to be buried or cremated, notice the people in attendance and observe your feelings and sensations. Repeating this imaginary scene in detail will heighten your ability to consciously take in experiences beyond the death of the body. In response, you may cease to identify so strongly with the body and become more certain that death of the body is not death of you. With further practice, you may come to know that the being who is watching your corpse is your real self.

The world's great religions—among them Judaism, Buddhism, Christianity, and Islam—all agree that our relationship to the source is essential, yet they depict it in different ways. In today's world, where the touch of a computer key connects us electronically to the entire world at once yet eliminates face-to-face contact and even telephone interactions, we must remember to see all concepts, including the passage from life to death, from a variety of viewpoints.

According to some religions, what we are thinking when we die is highly significant. For this reason, devout practitioners try to fill every moment with thoughts of God. If our mind is filled with God while we are alive, they say, when we die our mind will take us straight to God. Gandhi told his students the day before he died, "If the last words I speak before I die are not the name of God, then all

I have taught you is worth nothing." His last words were "Ram, Ram," the name of his god.

Other religions use different terms to describe the same phenomenon. In Tibetan Buddhism, the phases after life are called *bardos,* or in-between stages—transition points that can be very confusing to the recently deceased who are not prepared for them. Still other religions refer to a "waiting room" between this world and the next, where the deceased are expected to explain their actions on earth. What is said in this room influences where they will go next. Thus, amid all the religions in our world, as the Hermetica reminds us, there is but one spiritual decree: "Do not be evil." To avoid being evil, we must be acutely conscious of our actions and at all times aware of the presence of God.

How we prepare for death is up to us, but prepare we must, for in doing so we can enhance our quality of life. By developing a relationship with our god during our time on earth, we may be inspired to purify our intentions and learn to listen to our intuition, which in turn will keep us filled with good ideas and a sense of right action. By remembering that in the end we all die, that in a hundred years no one will know who we were, we may realize that our errors will be forgotten along with our accomplishments. We may then regard death as the ultimate redeemer delivering us from the pain and guilt wrought by our errors.

Preparing for death as we live allows us to free ourselves of guilt by accepting our humanity and by understanding that errors are part of our learning process. We can then pursue self-improvement with great zest, all the while remaining conscious of our actions yet unattached to the results. In this way we keep moving forward in search of our essence.

The search for ultimate truth, our reason for being, and our essence, is a journey to awakening. This illuminating quest is encapsulated in the following Sufi story of a seeker.

A man who believed that normal, everyday life could not possibly be the reason for existence set off in search of a teacher. As the years passed, he read many books, attended several schools, and met one master after another. He worked with the spiritual practices that appealed to him the most. Some of his experiences brought him great peace whereas others brought only feelings of emptiness. He had no idea how evolved he was or when his search might end.

One day, the man was thinking about his life when he suddenly found himself near the house of a well-known sage. In the sage's garden he encountered Khidr, secret guide of the Sufis, who shows the way to truth. Khidr took the man to a place filled with people in great distress. When he asked who they were, they said, "We are those who did not follow real teachings and who were not sincere about our motivation."

Khidr then took the man to a place where everyone was happily partying. When he asked who they were, they replied, "We are those who did not follow the signs for the path to truth."

"But if you ignored the signs, how can you be happy?" asked the man.

"Because we chose happiness instead of truth," said the people.

"But is happiness not the goal of all people?" asked the seeker.

"The goal is truth. Truth is greater than happiness. Those who know truth can have whatever mood they choose, or none," they told him. "We convinced ourselves that truth is happiness and happiness truth, and people believed us; you, too, have until now imagined that happiness must be the same as truth. But happiness makes you its prisoner, as does suffering."

The man then found himself back in the garden, with Khidr beside him. "I will grant you one wish," said Khidr.

"I wish to know why I have thus far failed in my search and how I can achieve my goal of knowing God," the man replied.

"You have all but wasted your life," said Khidr, "because you have lied to yourself. You have been satisfying your desire for pleasure and avoiding pain, when you could have been seeking truth."

"And yet I met you," said the man, "and that rarely happens to anyone."

"And you met me," said Khidr, "because you had sufficient sincerity to desire truth for its own sake, at least for an instant. It was your sincerity that brought me to you."

Now the man felt an overwhelming desire to find truth, even if he lost himself in the process.

Khidr started to walk away, whereupon the man began to run after him. "You may not follow me," said Khidr, "because I am returning to the ordinary world—the world of lies—for that is where I must be if I am to do my work."

Looking around, the man realized that he was no longer in the sage's garden, but rather in the Land of Truth.

Finding truth, we may realize how very balanced ordinary life can be. As Gandhi put it: "A life without truth is a life I would rather not live."

And there, in the Land of Truth, may you find all the success and joys of this life and the next, whatever they may be.

IF

If you can keep your head when all about you
Are losing theirs and blaming it on you;
If you can trust yourself when all men doubt you,
But make allowance for their doubting too;

If you can wait and not be tired by waiting,
Or, being lied about, don't deal in lies,
Or, being hated, don't give way to hating,
And yet don't look too good, nor talk too wise;

If you can dream—and not make dreams your master;
If you can think—and not make thoughts your aim;
If you can meet with triumph and disaster
And treat those two imposters just the same;

If you can bear to hear the truth you've spoken
Twisted by knaves to make a trap for fools,
Or watch the things you gave your life to broken,
And stoop and build 'em up with wornout tools;

If you can make one heap of all your winnings
And risk it on one turn of pitch-and-toss,
And lose, and start again at your beginnings
And never breathe a word about your loss;

If you can force your heart and nerve and sinew
To serve your turn long after they are gone,
And so hold on when there is nothing in you
Except the Will which says to them: "Hold on";

If you can talk with crowds and keep your virtue,
Or walk with kings—nor lose the common touch;

If neither foes nor loving friends can hurt you;
If all men count with you, but none too much;

If you can fill the unforgiving minute
With sixty seconds' worth of distance run—
Yours is the Earth and everything that's in it,
And—which is more—you'll be a Man, my son!

– Rudyard Kipling

Bibliography

Attenborough, Richard. *Mohandas K. Gandhi: The Words of Gandhi*. New York: New Market Press, 1982.

Bennett, J. G. *Is There "Life" on Earth? An Introduction to Gurdjieff*. New York: Stonehill, 1973.

Copenhaver, Brian P. *Hermetica: The Greek Corpus Hermeticum and the Latin Asclepius*. Cambridge, England: Cambridge University Press, 1992.

Eliade, Mircea. *Yoga: Immortality and Freedom*. Princeton, NJ: Princeton University Press, 1958.

Gibran, Kahlil. *The Prophet*. New York: Alfred A. Knopf, 1923.

Gurdjieff, G. I. *Beelzebub's Tales to His Grandson: All and Everything*. New York: Arkana, 1992.

Gurdjieff, G. I. *Life Is Real Only Then, When "I Am": All and Everything*. New York: Arkana, 1991.

Gurdjieff, G. I. *Meetings with Remarkable Men: All and Everything*. New York: Arkana, 1991.

Hill, Napoleon. *Think and Grow Rich*. Bombay, India: D. B. Taraporevala Sons & Company, 1940.

The Impersonal Life. Marina del Rey, CA: DeVorss & Company, 1969.

Jonas, Hans. *The Gnostic Religion: The Message of the Alien God and the Beginnings of Christianity*. Boston: Beacon Press, 1958.

Kaplan, Aryeh. *Meditation and Kabbalah*. York Beach, ME: Samuel Weiser, 1982.

Krishnamurti, J. *The Flame of Attention*. San Francisco: Harper & Row, 1984.

Levine, Stephen. *A Gradual Awakening*. New York: Doubleday, 1979.

Lo, Benjamin Pang Jeng, et al. *The Essence of T'ai Chi Ch'uan: The Literary Tradition*. Berkeley, CA: North Atlantic Books, 1979.

Ouspensky, P. D. *Fourth Way*. New York: Random House, 1971.

Ouspensky, P. D. *The Psychology of Man's Possible Evolution*. New York: Random House, 1981.

Ouspensky, P. D. *In Search of the Miraculous: Fragments of an Unknown Teaching*. New York: Harcourt Brace Jovanovich, 1949.

Ozak, Muzaffer. *Love Is the Wine: Talks of a Sufi Master.* Brattleboro, VT: Threshold Books, 1987.

Rinpoche, Sogyal. *The Tibetan Book of Living and Dying.* New York: HarperCollins, 1993.

Scott, Walter. *Hermetica: The Ancient Greek and Latin Writings Which Contain Religious or Philosophic Teachings Ascribed to Hermes Trismegistus.* Kila, MT: Kessinger Publishing Company, 1926.

Seven Taoist Masters: A Folk Novel of China. Trans. by Eva Wong. Boston: Shambhala Publications, 1990.

Steiner, Rudolf. *How to Know Higher Worlds.* Spring Valley, NY: The Anthroposophic Press, 1994.

T'ai Chi Classics. Trans. by Waysun Liao. Boston: Shambhala Publications, 1990.

The Tibetan Book of the Dead. Trans. by Francesca Fremantle and Chogyam Trungpa. Boston: Shambhala Publications, 1992.

Wing, R. L. *The Tao of Power.* New York: Doubleday & Company, 1986.

Yogi Ramacharaka. *Advanced Course in Yogi Philosophy and Oriental Occultism.* Chicago: The Yogi Publication Society, 1904.

About the Author

David Samuel was born in Montreal, Canada, to a mother from Bombay and a father from Baghdad. After starting his first business at age thirteen, he went on to develop eight companies and retire by age twenty-eight—a feat he attributes to the spiritual teachings that infused his business practices. Upon retiring, he began to travel throughout the Far and Middle East, devoting several years to the study of the regions' mystical teachings.

Settling in Colorado, David integrated his business and spiritual philosophies into a system of learning currently taught at The Institute of Practical Mysticism, which he founded in 1996. Currently, he works with international research and development projects focused on environmentally sound technologies as well as cures for life-threatening illnesses.

Order Form

Quantity		Amount
_____	*Practical Mysticism: Business Success and Balanced Living*	
	Through Ancient and Modern Spiritual Teachings ($14.95)	_____
	Sales tax of 7% for Colorado residents	_____
	Shipping & handling ($3.00 for first book;	
	$1.50 for each additional book)	_____
	Total amount enclosed	_____

Quantity discounts available.

Please contact your local bookstore or mail your order, together with your name, address, and personal check or money order, to:

BP

Bakshi Publications, LLC
283 Columbine Street, Suite 123
Denver, CO 80206

To order by phone, call The Institute of Practical Mysticism:
1-877-MYSTIC-0 (877-697-8420)
For credit card orders, call:
1-800-507-BOOK

Please send queries, comments, or requests for information to The Institute of Practical Mysticism at the address listed above.